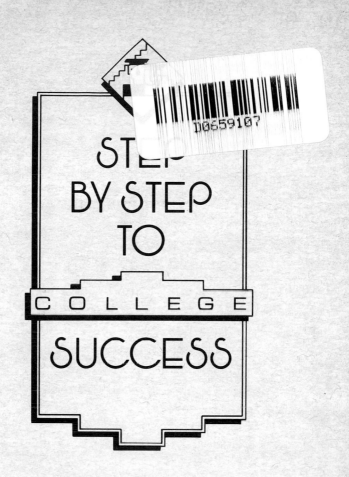

STEP
BY STEP
TO

COLLEGE

SUCCESS

STEP
BY STEP
TO
COLLEGE
SUCCESS

A. JEROME JEWLER
Co-director, University 101 Freshman Seminar Program
Professor of Journalism
University of South Carolina, Columbia

JOHN N. GARDNER
Director, University 101 Freshman Seminar Program
Associate Vice President
for University Campuses and Continuing Education
Professor of Library and Information Science
University of South Carolina, Columbia

Wadsworth Publishing Company • Belmont, California • A Division of Wadsworth, Inc.

ENGLISH EDITOR John Strohmeier
EDITORIAL ASSISTANTS Holly Allen, Sharon McNally
PRODUCTION EDITOR Harold Humphrey
TEXT AND COVER DESIGNER Julia Scannell
PRINT BUYER Karen Hunt
COPY EDITOR Linda Purrington
COMPOSITOR Kachina Typesetting, Inc.
SIGNING REPRESENTATIVE Susan Wilson

Printed in the United States of America

2 3 4 5 6 7 8 9 10——91 90 89 88 87

Library of Congress Cataloging-in-Publication Data

Jewler, A. Jerome.
   Step by step to college success.

   1. College student orientation.   2. College
freshman—United States.   3. Study, Method of.
4. Academic achievement.   I. Gardner, John N.
II. Title.
LB2343.32.J48   1987   378'.18   86-24729
ISBN 0-534-07998-9

This book could not have been possible without the assistance of our many colleagues in the University 101 program at the University of South Carolina and elsewhere, who made major contributions to our earlier work, *College Is Only the Beginning*. We would therefore like to thank Ed Ewing, Charles Curran, Jim Burns, Linda Salane, Barbara Alley, Jim Lancaster, Ray Edwards, Richard Wertz, Mary Beth Love, Ruthann Fox-Hines, Kevin King, Randy Lamkin, Linda Morphis, Mike Shaver, Tom Shandley, Mark Shanley, Dennis Pruitt, and Hilda Owens. Again, we thank Belle Jewler and Donna Gardner for giving us the time to develop this new volume of sage advice for entering college students. We are grateful to Frances Rauschenberg of the University of Georgia and Dr. John Lewis of West Georgia College, who reviewed the manuscript and made helpful suggestions.

PREFACE

A GUIDE TO THE FIVE JOURNEYS IN THIS BOOK

Among the famous pathways of our time, there's the yellow brick road, the road to ruin, the primrose path, and easy street. This journey is something else entirely. It's a step-by-step route through one of the most significant events in your life: the freshman year of college.

What makes the freshman year such a milestone in the lives of individuals? As you follow the path through these pages, you will find out. But for now, let us simply say that those of you who choose college are also choosing a plan for the rest of your lives. In college, you will have the time to learn to live on your own for perhaps the first time in your life. In college, you will be making decisions you have never had to make before. In college, you'll be meeting people from all walks of life, from different cultural backgrounds, from different parts of America and the world. In college, you will be taught by men and women who are acknowledged specialists in their fields, and many probably won't come from your hometown or even your home state. College will offer you the opportunity to grow dynamically in at least six directions at once: intellectually, vocationally, emotionally, spiritually, physically, and socially. That isn't an easy task by any means, and it helps to have a plan. This book is intended to help you develop that plan.

The idea behind this book, therefore, is really a very simple one. It is that college, like all things in life, works best when you are prepared to reap all its rewards and benefits. We who have put this little volume together have been dedicated to helping freshmen succeed in college for a combined total of nearly forty years. We administer the best-known freshman seminar course in the country. With this experience behind us, and as former freshmen ourselves, we're in a position to offer sound advice to those of you who are just now thinking about college, or who are just about to begin your freshman year.

Our advice, in a nutshell, is this:

First, be certain you understand why you're going to college. Learn to develop a positive attitude toward learning, one you can fully believe in and can become genuinely excited about.

Next, clarify your needs. Be absolutely certain you know what you need to get out of college.

Then, use those needs as a plan to obtain the most from your college years.

It can be done, and you can do it! And doing it right can make the difference between just going through the motions of going to college, and getting all from college that college has to offer—a whole lot more, by the way, than most college students ever receive.

If you're reading this book on your own, read at your leisure and work through some of the suggested exercises. If you're reading it as part of a group or class, become involved with your group in as many activities as possible.

Now, here's your road map. This book is divided into five trips, or journeys. Each journey consists of a number of small steps. We emphasize "small" because the best learning takes place when it's organized into small steps or chunks.

The first journey is called, appropriately, "Preparing for the Rest of the Trip." Just as you need to pack and make other plans for a real journey, so you need to make preparations for this one.

The second journey is called "Setting the Stage for Learning to Take Place." We know the best learning takes place when students are in a learning environment that makes them eager to learn and eager to participate in that learning, and where there is a bond of trust between teacher and learner. That's why this journey will take you through a series of steps designed to build a sense of community in the classroom.

Only when you feel that good about learning can you make the most out of the three remaining trips. The third trip, "Discovering What a Freshman Needs to Know Most," is the basis for everything that follows. Steps in this journey will help you determine what you really need to know, what skills you need to sharpen, and how to begin planning for the years ahead. It's one of the most important journeys, so take it slowly, and make the most of it.

The fourth trip, "Finding the Answers," is one in which you'll be making many stops along the way. All around you, all over your campus, are the people, the facilities, the resources, and the groups to help you get what you need and to aid in your total development, not only as a student, but as a human being.

Finally, you'll embark on your fifth and final trip, "Becoming Responsible for Your Personal Growth." You'll look back on what you have done and where you have been, and reflect on what you've gained, how you've grown, and what lies ahead.

We have already suggested that, as authors of this book, we are well qualified professionally to provide this advice. What we need to add is that we were once college freshmen, too, and each of us, in our own way, experienced a freshman year filled with frustration and misery, emotions which, fortunately, were replaced by enthusiasm, excitement, and love of learning and of our newfound life situations.

It almost caused at least one of us to drop out forever. While you're wondering which of us that was, we think it's time you began your journey.

A. Jerome Jewler
John N. Gardner
January 1987

CONTENTS

PREFACE   A GUIDE TO THE FIVE JOURNEYS IN THIS BOOK   vii

JOURNEY ONE
PREPARING FOR THE REST OF THE TRIP   3

STEP 1   5
Discover Your Own Reasons for Going to College

EXERCISE Suggested Follow-up   6

STEP 2   7
Now See What Others Say about the
Value of College

EXERCISE 1 Second Draft   12
EXERCISE 2 College Fears   13
EXERCISE 3 What Is Higher Education? Things to Think About   15

JOURNEY TWO
SETTING THE STAGE FOR LEARNING TO TAKE PLACE   19

STEP 3   23
Find Out How College Is Different from High School

EXERCISE 1 How College May Differ from High School   29
EXERCISE 2 What I Liked about High School   29
EXERCISE 3 Computing a Grade-Point Average   29

STEP 4   31
Join a Group. Discover What You Are and Who They Are.

EXERCISE 1 The Strengths Exercise   34
EXERCISE 2 How You Developed Your Values   36
EXERCISE 3 A Values-Based Interview   36
EXERCISE 4 Another Way of Declaring Your Values   37
EXERCISE 5 The Choice   37

STEP 5   41
Realize That Your Professors Are People Who Once Were Freshmen, Too

EXERCISE 1 Interviewing a Professor   51

JOURNEY THREE
DISCOVERING WHAT A FRESHMAN NEEDS TO KNOW MOST

53

STEP 6   55
Writing Effectively. The Key to Discovery.

EXERCISE 1 Writing about Writing   60
EXERCISE 2 Nonstop Freewriting   61
EXERCISE 3 Looping   61

STEP 7   63
Learn How to Speak "College"

STEP 8   65
Learn What's Out There for You
    EXERCISE 1 Needs and Resources. Making a Match.   72

JOURNEY FOUR
FINDING THE ANSWERS

FINDING THE ANSWERS   75

STEP 9   77
How to Improve Your Study Skills
    EXERCISE 1 Choosing Study Methods   85
    EXERCISE 2 Group Sharing of Study Methods   85

STEP 10   87
Your Academic Advisor. The Person with
the Answers.
    EXERCISE 1 Rating Your Advisor   94
    EXERCISE 2 Giving Thanks Where Thanks Are Due   95
    EXERCISE 3 Shaping the Ideal Advisor Relationship   96

STEP 11   97
Your Academic Major, Your Future Career
    EXERCISE 1 Field Research on Careers and Majors   104
    EXERCISE 2 Personality Mosaic   104

STEP 12   111
Using Your College Library for Better Papers,
Enhanced Learning, and Higher Grades
    EXERCISE 1 The Library Search, from A to Z   115

STEP 13 121
Finding the Money for College. Managing It After You Get There.

EXERCISE 1 Constructing Your Personal Budget 129
EXERCISE 2 Steps in Applying for Financial Aid 132

STEP 14 133
Becoming More Comfortable with Yourself and Others

EXERCISE 1 A Brief Relaxation Exercise 141
EXERCISE 2 Discovering Your Campus Counseling Center 142
EXERCISE 3 Identifying Behaviors 142

STEP 15 145
When You Feel Your Best, You Do Your Best

EXERCISE 1 Breaking the Pattern 150
EXERCISE 2 Breaking into an Exercise Routine 150

STEP 16 151
Alcohol, Drugs, and the Issue of Responsibility

EXERCISE 1 Alcohol. Facts vs. Myths. 159

STEP 17 163
Making It Feel Like Home

EXERCISE 1 Comparing Living Options 168
EXERCISE 2 Learning about Other Lifestyles 168

STEP 18 169
Avoiding that Left-Out Feeling. Activities and Leadership.

EXERCISE 1 Relating Activities to Personal Development 174
EXERCISE 2 Learning Leadership Skills Firsthand 175
EXERCISE 3 A Class Survey of Campus Activities 175

JOURNEY FIVE
BECOMING RESPONSIBLE FOR YOUR PERSONAL GROWTH   177

STEP 19   179
Successfully Completing Your Freshman Year.
Options.

EXERCISE 1 Setting Goals for the Future   184
EXERCISE 2 A Fantasy Trip into the Future   185

GLOSSARY   187

STEP
BY STEP
TO

COLLEGE

SUCCESS

JOURNEY ONE

PREPARING FOR THE REST OF THE TRIP

One of our basic assumptions about both traveling and learning is that it always helps to know where you're going and why you're going there. That's why we begin our adventure by asking you to, literally, take the first step. Once you've done that, we'll provide you with some additional and, we believe, surprising information about the value of college, and we'll follow that with some activities that will help you get a firmer grasp on who you are, what you want out of college, and what you expect to derive from the many life experiences still awaiting you.

One word of caution: Please don't jump ahead to the second step until you have completed the first. That's sort of the rule of thumb in this book. If you skip steps, or jump haphazardly through this book and meander back and forth along the route, we can't promise you'll reach your destination in optimum condition!

Trust us! And turn the page to begin.

STEP 1

DISCOVER YOUR OWN REASONS FOR GOING TO COLLEGE

Throughout this book we'll be asking you to do a great deal of writing. We want to point out at the very start that you should not approach such assignments as if they were going to be turned in for a grade. We'll have much more to say about writing later, but for now, we want to make it very clear that this particular exercise (as well as many others in this book) is primarily for *you*. If you are a member of a freshman seminar class, it would be helpful to share this paper with other students, who in turn would share their thoughts with you. This exchange of thinking among students, by the way, is one very good way for learning to take place.

So find a comfortable spot, get some paper and a pen, and begin writing, in your own words, and in your own style, about how you made the decision to attend a college, and specifically, the college you have chosen (if you have made that decision). Think about all the advantages of someone with a college education (you) over someone who does not attend college, and include these assumptions in your writing. Don't work hard to make this a formal essay. On the contrary, have some fun with this assignment. Allow your thoughts to ramble, and put all your thoughts down on paper, even though many of them may seem silly or insignificant. Remember, no one has to see this paper except you, so be more concerned with what you say than the manner in which you say it.

Ready? Relax and start writing. Remember, your thoughts should focus on how you want college to make a difference in your life.

If appropriate, bring your paper to class and share it aloud with others as they share theirs with you and others in the class. This works best in small discussion groups of five to seven people. After everyone in each group has taken the time to share his or her thoughts, one member of each group should report back to the entire class and cover the major thoughts and feelings expressed by members of the group. What did others in the group have in common? What were some of the differences? How did this make you feel about your connection to this group? It may be helpful to write major points for each group on a large easel pad.

STEP 2

NOW SEE WHAT OTHERS SAY ABOUT THE VALUE OF COLLEGE

In our earlier book, *College Is Only the Beginning*, college professor and administrator Hilda F. Owens explained the difference college can make. She reported that many wonderful, challenging, and satisfying experiences would accrue to the fortunate individuals who chose to work toward a college degree. On the other hand, she warned that going to college could also be a stressful and frustrating experience.

You should know that you may experience what some call "cognitive dissonance," or resistance to ideas which are foreign to you. This exposure is essential for further learning and development. If you were not exposed to new ideas which proved challenging and often disturbing to you, how on earth could you become better educated?

Notwithstanding the fact that this risk is there, it appears that the good outweighs the bad in the college experience. For example, studies indicate that students in college tend to be more accepting of new ideas and more able to control their own destinies. What's more, they feel better about themselves (self-esteem), display a greater appreciation for the cultural and esthetic values of life, and are better able to grasp broad theoretical issues.

But the news is even better. From all the evidence to date, colleges seem to do a very good job at what they claim to do best: increase the knowledge and development of their students. Furthermore, educational achievement has a very definite positive correlation with career opportunities and income level. In an age when many are questioning the investment of time and money in a college education, evidence still shows that it is a sound investment.

As one educator has expressed it, "If you think education is expensive, try ignorance."

Students tend to leave college not only more competent, but more *confident*. They tend to have a better sense of who they are, where they fit in the scheme of things, and how they might make a difference in the world about them. You can expect to experience changes in your attitudes, values, behaviors, and self-concepts as a result of college, but mostly in positive directions.

So why are college graduates generally more able to adapt to most future situations than those who didn't attend college? Among the reasons are that they tend to adopt more liberal views, develop greater interest in political and public affairs, are more likely to vote and be active in community affairs, and are less likely to lead a life of crime.

College also helps people develop the flexibility, mobility, and knowledge needed to adapt to the changing demands of work and life. It also seems to contribute to increased on-the-job productivity and satisfaction.

But college offers even more. It is an important influence on family life. As women earn more of the family income, matters of child care and household responsibilities tend to be shared by husband and wife. College graduates tend to delay the age of marriage, have fewer children, and spend more time, thought, energy, and money on child rearing. They also tend to divorce less, and their children seem to have greater abilities and to enjoy greater achievements of their own than other children.

College-educated people tend to save more of their money, take greater but wiser investment risks, and spend considerably more on their homes, intellectual and cultural interests, and their children. They also tend to spend more wisely in the marketplace, and are better able, because of their education, to deal with misleading advertising, tax laws, and the legal system.

They spend less time and money on television and movies and more time on intellectual and cultural pursuits, including adult education, hobbies, community and civic affairs, and vacations.

College graduates are also likely to be more concerned with the prevention, rather than just treatment, of physical and mental health matters. Diet, exercise, stress management, and other factors result in longer life spans and fewer disabilities. Attention to health is probably related to an increased self-concept and sense of personal worth.

Perhaps Kingman Brewster, a former president of Yale University, said it best when asked to define the primary goals of a college education. He claimed those goals consisted of the development of three senses: a sense of place, a sense of self, and a sense of judgment. Brewster clearly argued for the broader and more liberating view of education when he concluded:

The most fundamental value of education is that it makes life more interesting. This is true whether you are fetched up on a desert island or adrift in the impersonal loneliness of the urban hurly-burley. It allows you to see things which the uneducated do not see. It allows you to understand things which do not occur to the less learned. In short, it makes it less likely that you will be bored with life. It also makes it less likely that you will be a crashing bore to those whose company you keep. By analogy, it makes the difference between the traveler who understands the local language and the traveler to whom the local language is a jumble of nonsense words.[1]

As you are begining to see, the college experience can provide so much more than intellectual development. In truth, it offers individuals such as yourself an opportunity for no less than six areas of development, of which the intellect is but one.

---

1. Davis, J.R. *Going to College: The Study of Students and the Student Experience*. Boulder, Colo.: Westview Press, 1977. p.xv.

Let's review those areas. We ask that you become familiar with them, because in the steps and journeys which follow, you'll be meeting them again and again. The six areas of development are intellectual, occupational, emotional, physical, social, and spiritual.

What is *intellectual development?* Quite frankly, it's much more than memorizing a set of facts so that you can pass an exam. A good instructor and a dedicated learner want much more than this to transpire in and out of the classroom. Intellectual development, then, means that you will learn how to create ideas in your own words and express them to others; to interpret readings and lectures and make sense out of what is being communicated in them; to communicate to others in a manner which is sensible, logical, and clear (whether in discussion or writing); and to understand and appreciate the significance of the learning process and realize that it is one of the great joys in life.

And what of *occupational development?* Educators everywhere are arguing about whether the purpose of college is to provide a broad education or intensive career training. We say it must do both. To us, occupational development means not only assistance on career planning and awareness of the opportunities in the world of work that fit a student's interests and abilities, but also a further appreciation of how the liberal arts and sciences provide thinking skills that are directly applicable to the great majority of career fields.

Emotional development is another important aspect of college. It refers to helping students learn to cope with stress and anxiety, become aware of their own feelings, and feel positive and enthusiastic about life, about aspirations, and about their abilities to achieve.

Physical development simply means that one of the goals of college is to impress upon students the lifelong value of fitness, exercise, and nutrition, as well as the risks of alcohol and drug abuse.

Social development reminds us that no man or woman is an island, and that each of us must learn the value of contributing to the common welfare of the community in which we exist. Getting along with others and gaining their support goes a long way toward enriching the lives of each of us. These same social skills will also help us function much better in work groups throughout college and throughout our working careers.

Finally, *spiritual development* means gaining a sense of one's own values as well as an appreciation of the value systems of others, having a sense of ethics, and a general appreciation of life and the natural forces in the universe. In other words, if you understand the purpose of your life and why you are here, you tend not only to feel better about yourself, but also to work better with others who may not share your views.

Perhaps the greatest lesson in personal development, however, stems from the realization that all six of these areas have major impacts on one another, and therefore on the growth of the individual. Let's look at an example. One of your authors, Jerry Jewler, is an active writer, teacher, administrator, and speaker because he has developed an enthusiasm for learning and literally loves the kinds of work he is called upon to do. (Oh, he gripes and grumbles now and then, but through education, he has found his calling.) One reason he can enjoy his work and not let it get him down is his devotion to exercise. He swims three or four times weekly, spurred on not only by his realization that exercise keeps both mind and body in optimum condition, but also by the fact that he underwent coronary bypass surgery in 1983 and this is his way of keeping himself in top physical/mental/emotional shape.

He made major strides in his occupational development while attending college, where he majored in journalism. This led to a career in advertising, a subsequent career in teaching advertising on a college campus, and a second career in freshman education. His emotional development consists of a lifelong dedication to avoiding stressful situations, knowing when to "call it a day," and discovering that what seems monumentally impossible for the moment is never quite as foreboding the next day. He is quite positive (and vocal!) about his beliefs (spiritual development), but works hard to appreciate the differing opinions of others. Although he feels he works best alone, he enjoys the company of others and is stimulated intellectually by meaningful discussions with them.

The point is that you can construct such an interlocking portrait of yourself, calling on all six areas, and discovering that strength and self-esteem in one leads to similar strengths in the others.

For all of this is what we mean by "education." Students who are physically unfit won't perform at their intellectual best. Occupationally confused students (in the wrong major, for example), may feel that confusion extending to other areas of their lives, and those who aren't certain of their own personal values and are unwilling to accept the values of others may find it difficult to deal with society.

College, then, is much more than just a place where learning happens in the classroom. Many students, unfortunately, fail to realize this, and although their grades are impressive, they never realize their full potential because their education starts and stops with the ringing of the bell. We have a profoundly different idea about learning and college. We believe, first, that learning is a lifelong process and that college is where it can blossom. We further believe that an educated person is a person who has grown in all six of the dimensions we have discussed. Finally, we declare that the day you stop learning, that day you stop living.

That's why we believe the college experience is a way for everyone to improve his or her lot in life.

And as more of us experience college, how can life be anything but better?

EXERCISE 1
SECOND DRAFT

Using your paper about how and why you chose your college as a basis, and incorporating thoughts from what you have just read, write a second draft. If you quote information from what you have just been reading in this book, be certain you mention this as a source. This is known as citing a reference, and it helps your reader understand the source of your comments. As part of the paper, apply the six areas of development to yourself, and imagine what you want to do to improve each area and how each of those activities might affect every other area of your growth. If the opportunity arises, share these thoughts with others in your class in a small-group setting.

■ EXERCISE 2

COLLEGE FEARS

Here is a list of the most common fears as reported by freshmen during their first week of college. Check the ones you are experiencing or feel you will be experiencing. Add other fears you may have (this list is by no means complete!).

_____ I will not have enough money to do all the things I want to do.

_____ I will not be able to manage my time for studying, sleeping, meals, and so forth.

_____ I will have difficulty meeting friends.

_____ I will have difficulty in relationships with the opposite sex.

_____ I will become depressed, and this will affect my ability to make good grades.

_____ College will be too difficult for me.

_____ I don't feel I belong in college.

_____ I will disappoint my parents because of my low grades.

_____ I will have trouble getting along with my roommate.

_____ I will get lost on campus.

_____ I will have difficulty finding a major I like.

_____ I will choose a major which is not suited to my skills or interests.

_____ I will become homesick, and this will affect my grades.

_____ I will not be able to develop proper study habits, and this will affect my grades.

_____ I will have trouble understanding professors, and this will affect my grades.

____ I will be looked upon by others as an inferior person.

____ I will be too shy to express my true feelings to others.

____ I will be tempted to cheat in class in order to get good grades.

____ I will not appear as sophisticated as other freshmen.

Now add to this list with other fears you have that we haven't included, plus other fears of students you know:

_____

_____

_____

_____

_____

_____

Now read what the freshmen we talked with told us they fear *most*:

- I will not be able to manage my time.
- I will become depressed and this will affect my performance in class.
- College will be too difficult for me.
- I will become homesick.
- I will not be able to develop proper study habits.
- I will have trouble understanding the professor.

Other responses included:

- I will gain weight.

- I won't be able to write essays.

- I will have to choose from too many clubs and too many hard classes.

- I will not be able to compete with upperclass students in my classes.

- I'm from another part of the country and it will be hard to make friends. They won't understand me.

- I already have $15 in parking tickets.

- I won't have time to play tennis.

- I won't have time to work on the student newspaper.

As you can see, freshmen have many concerns, and you should not feel strange if you have these and others. It's a good idea to share these fears in class. List the ones that most concern you on a piece of paper, without adding your name. Your instructor or class members can then report on those fears which were expressed most frequently, and then your discussion can turn to how to go about resolving those fears. Later in this book, we'll help you identify places and people on your campus who can help. For the time being, we would like you to go back over your list and ours, and attempt to assign one of the six development areas to each fear. For example, worrying about making friends is social. Fear of weight gain is physical. Fear that others won't understand you is social and spiritual (differing values). Classifying your concerns is also a way of clarifying them, and is the first step toward finding a way to be rid of them for good.

■ EXERCISE 3

WHAT IS HIGHER EDUCATION?
THINGS TO THINK ABOUT

Throughout college and life, you will be asked to revise your thinking about many things. Some of these new ideas may appear strange to you at first. But remember what we said earlier: You need to confront new ideas and try to understand them in order to grow intellectually. This does not mean, by the way, that you need to accept them all! That would certainly miss the entire point of learning. The five statements below were made by educators who take a rather liberal view of education. Do you agree with them? Do you disagree? And why? Remember, everyone is entitled to an opinion, but you should be able to support your argument with logical thoughts. Take a moment to read through the five statements. Then choosing one or more, write a short paper in which you agree or disagree. List your reasons for feeling as you do. Then share your views in class with others. Don't argue too much with someone who disagrees with you. Simply listen to the other side of the question. After you have had a chance to share your feelings with others, the class should discuss how this helped clarify for them the purpose of higher education. What did you learn about the purpose of higher education from this exercise?

1. Years ago, college was only for a select group of people. Today, we urge everyone to try to get a college education, even if they are not fully prepared for it. As a result, a college education is more valuable to us than before.

2. Years ago, people who attended college were more interested in getting a liberal education (learning how to think about new things) than in preparing for careers. Today, students seem to be more interested in learning the specific skills they will need for their chosen careers. As a result, college graduates are better off than before.

3. Years ago, colleges allowed students to sink or swim on their own in the belief that those who were college material would make it through. Today we have advisement programs, orientation programs, special freshman seminars, career and counseling centers, and more. As a result, college students are more able to make it on their own when they graduate.

4. Grades, tests, and lectures interfere with the learning process. Get rid of them, and real learning will take place. (What would you do in place of grades, tests, and lectures?)

5. Teaching isn't just throwing information at students and hoping they will remember it for the quiz. In a true learning environment, teachers and students are learning from one another and share the role of "information giver." (What is an information giver, how can teachers learn from students, and why does this tend to make it easier for students to learn?)

Congratulations. You have just completed your maiden voyage. In a short space of time, you have made some decisions about why college is important for you, and you have learned what others have said about the value of college. If you've done everything we've asked of you so far, you have prepared yourself for the balance of this trip. In Journey II, you will find yourself making closer ties to your new college environment. It's time to begin that journey now.

JOURNEY TWO

SETTING THE STAGE
FOR LEARNING
TO TAKE PLACE

We'd like to begin this journey with a thought and a suggestion. The thought is this: that learning is much more enjoyable and, therefore, more interesting when the learner, or student, is allowed to actively participate in the learning process. Think for a moment about the classes you enjoyed most in high school and the classes you learned the most in. Chances are they were one and the same. And we're willing to bet that, in those courses, you were fortunate enough to have teachers who called on you frequently, who demanded that you speak up in class and contribute to the discussion, and who made it easy and yet challenging for you to do so. This is what we call "interactive learning," and it only happens when the student is allowed to be an information *giver* as well as an information *receiver*. What's more, the professors who ask you to contribute something to the class aren't doing it out of laziness on their part. On the contrary, they've worked hard to provide you with time to have your say. They learn from you, your fellow students learn from you, and you learn from your professor and the other students in the room.

So much for the thought. The suggestion has to do with creating an environment in the classroom where this type of learning can take place. So if you're reading this as part of a class or other group, here's what we want you to do. If you're not already sitting in a circle, move your chairs! Arrange them in one large circle and get rid of any empty chairs so that the circle will be as small and as tight as your group can make it. Now that you have one large circle, where everyone can see everyone else and nobody is in the back of the room (because there is no longer a back of the room), we want you to begin getting comfortable with one another. One person begins by introducing him- or herself, and tells about one thing he or she enjoys doing. The person to that person's right will reintroduce the first and re-mind the group of what that first person enjoys doing, then will introduce him- or herself in the same manner. The person on her right repeats the introductions, beginning once more with the original person. You will see the anxiety build and the laughter grow louder as the exercise begins to come full circle and the last person wonders if he or she will remember all the names and interesting comments. If you want to make this easier, instruct each person to introduce only the two people to the right. In any event, you will leave the class remembering the names and interests of most of the people in the room, even if you didn't know them before.

What does this "name chain" exercise accomplish? We view it as a wonderful way to break the ice on the opening day of class, to find out who others are, and perhaps to discover you share some of their interests. You might go around again and ask each person to state his or her hometown. If you do, chances are you will discover other freshmen who either live in your town or not too far away.

We hope that, through the name chain, you will discover what you and other people in your group have in common. More importantly, we believe you will also begin to make some decisions about which of these people you would like to know better. By the way, the instructor should participate too!

Now that you feel more comfortable, you're ready to take the next step.

STEP 3

FIND OUT HOW COLLEGE IS DIFFERENT FROM HIGH SCHOOL

Quickly, can you come up with five or six ways in which college is different from high school? Let's see, you say. First of all, you have to pay to attend college. Also, you don't *have* to go to college, you have to *want* to go. If you decide you want to attend college, you have many choices: schools near home, schools far away; private or public universities; two-year or four-year institutions. You might even decide you want to study abroad!

But the differences hardly stop there. Not only does it cost just to attend classes, it also costs to have textbooks, a place to live and food to eat, and it costs to pursue the collegiate lifestyle.

Perhaps the most disturbing change for freshmen, however, is their newfound sense of freedom. With no mom or dad or older brother or sister to tell you when to study, how late you can stay out, or even where you can go and with whom, you're pretty much on your own. And that can be scary! As a matter of fact, we believe the biggest problem college students face is having too much freedom. Just imagine the decisions you will be facing daily:

Should I get up or skip class? Should I dress nicely or make a spectacle of myself? Eat breakfast or skip it? Study regularly or cram for exams? Eat good food or junk food? Drink responsibly or become a drunk or not drink at all? Use drugs or not use them? Make friends with Jean or Jim? Join a Greek organization or not?

Exercise or not? Sleep or not? Keep your room straight or live like a pig? Become intimately involved with someone or not? And if you do, worry about birth control or leave it to your partner? Choose your courses each semester, drop a course, see your academic advisor, choose a major, choose a career, choose a husband or wife—*STOP!!!*

Is it any wonder a freshman sometimes becomes overwhelmed?

But there's hope. And help. And help in college begins with orientation. You will either attend an orientation session the summer before you begin classes or the week before the fall semester starts. Generally, you'll be welcomed to campus, and before you know it you'll be talking to an academic advisor about the courses you should be taking during your first semester. Be aware, however, that no orientation program can provide all the answers before school begins. Often, you won't even know what you don't know until you begin classes!

If you're fortunate enough to be using this book as part of an orientation course or freshman seminar that lasts an entire semester, this is your golden opportunity to discover what you will need to know during your college career. Not too many years ago, freshman seminar courses were practically nonexistent, and college faculty generally agreed there was no point in teaching college freshmen "how to go to college." But many of the educators who said this failed to realize that the college and the freshman were changing. With more and more young people determined to gain a college education, many entering freshmen were the first in their families ever to attend college, and were not prepared for the experience. At the same time, colleges, in an effort to serve the needs of this diverse group, were offering a broader range of programs, which resulted in rules and requirements that were more complex than ever before.

Today, colleges and universities are realizing that college is a major developmental step in the lives of each of us who choose to pursue this route, and that not all development can take place within the confines of the classroom. Since many students, bewildered with the many choices they face, are unable to make the decisions they are called upon to make, the freshman seminar or freshman orientation course was developed to provide a road map of sorts for them, much as this book is a road map for you.

Rather than tell freshmen what choices to make, however, the founders of such courses felt it was extremely important to leave those decisions to the students, and to help them make the proper choices by:

1. Creating a support group in which students would feel comfortable about discussing the issues involved in making those decisions.

2. Providing reinforcement for those decisions through a trained instructor who could serve as a mentor for a group of such freshmen.

3. Allowing the students, as a group, to discuss the issues and help one another find the right answers.

4. Directing students to resources beyond the classroom for further aid in the decision-making process. These resources might be people, offices, services, or activities on the campus.

5. Providing "hands-on" experiences for students with many of the helping resources on campus.

6. Teaching some critical coping skills—time management, study skills, writing, library skills, etc.—to make it easier for students to accomplish their goals.

You will be exploring many of these resources in a later step of this book (Step 8). For now, we want to review only the procedures you will need to know "up front."

■ ADMISSION TO COLLEGE

Each college sets its own standards for admission, and these may change from year to year. Some colleges may even admit a student to one program, but deny him or her admission to another. Probably the best advice we can offer if you have not yet applied for

admission is to be aware of the application deadlines and requirements for admission to your chosen program, and apply early! At
our university, although admission to the university virtually
guarantees the freshman admission to most programs, each program has its own progression requirements. This means, for example, that a freshman in the College of Journalism at USC must
achieve an overall grade-point average that is considerably higher
than the one required for admission to the university. If he or she
fails to do so after one year, the college may deny the student
admission to the sophomore year of the program, although the
student will still be registered at the university and able to take
classes.

■ SATISFYING ACADEMIC REQUIREMENTS

Another thing you will need to remember about college is that each
program has its own set of academic requirements, and it is the
responsibility of the student to meet those requirements or no
degree will be granted. This is not as scary as it sounds, but students
should study and remember the requirements for their program as
early as possible. You should also find and meet your academic
advisor, the person who can guide you through this maze of rules
for the fours years or so that you are at the institution. The advisor
is typically a professor in the department you have chosen to major
in, but may also be a professional academic advisor who does
nothing but help students decide on courses for the coming semester and provide guidance for academic problems the students may
be facing. We'll have more to say about this unique person in Step
10. For now, we just want to urge you to introduce yourself to this
person as early as possible in your college career. If you don't
know who your academic advisor is, ask the department in which
you are registered.

■ GRADES AND GRADUATION

Your grade-point average (GPA), sometimes called a grade-point
ratio (GPR), is computed on the basis of the number of hours you

attempt during a term for credit. Each grade represents a certain number of points. At most colleges, the system works like this:

- A = 4 points
- B = 3 points
- C = 2 points
- D = 1 point
- F = 0 points

When you multiply the number of points for your grade by the number of credits for that course, you can determine the total points you have earned in that course. Add the points for all courses taken that term, then divide this total by the number of hours you attempted that term. This is your GPA or GPR.

■ ATTENDANCE POLICIES

Class attendance policies vary dramatically. For some reason, many college students believe they will always be allowed a certain number of "cuts" each term. Although some colleges allow you to miss class occasionally, their catalogs discuss excused and un-excused absences and never mention the word *cut*. Many more good reasons exist for attending a class than for missing one. First, many professors establish tougher attendance policies than the one in the catalog. Second, some professors say they never take attendance, but add that a majority of the material necessary for passing the course will be in the lectures. Third, it has been proven time and time again that a direct relationship exists between class attendance and how well you learn the material, and thus between attendance and the final grade you receive. Unless you're absolutely unable to be there, never miss the first few classes of the term. This is when your professor will announce his or her policies regarding attendance, requirements for passing the course, and other vital information. If you are ill and must miss a class, notify your professor or advisor. If you know in advance you will be missing a class, your professor will appreciate knowing in advance, too. The best advice we can give you about attendance is simply, "Never miss a single class unless it's absolutely necessary." While we realize that you will enjoy exercising your newfound freedom in college, we don't believe that missing class is the most sensible way to use that freedom. Remember, you are paying for your classes, so you're not only cheating yourself of the knowledge you would gain, but you're also tossing away part of something you have paid dearly for without ever trying it.

■ UNDERSTANDING YOUR DEGREE PROGRAM

Most degree programs consist of required courses in your major, required courses outside your major (usually in the liberal arts and sciences), a minor or cognate (a group of courses which supports your major and is approved by your advisor or dean), and a small number of "free electives" which are not required for your program but will count toward your degree. To determine the best courses for you to take when you are given that choice, we offer the following suggestions:

1. Talk to a student who is currently taking or has taken the course. Ask about course requirements, who teaches the course, tests, attendance policies, and the professor's grading system.

2. Go to the campus bookstore and skim through the books required.

3. Ask the faculty member teaching the course to describe the course to you.

4. Ask your academic advisor what he or she thinks of the value of the course.

You'll be facing many new decisions during your first semester in college. We've attempted to provide at least some of the answers for you in this step. As you progress through this journey and the subsequent ones, we'll begin to go into more detail about the many other things you'll need to know.

EXERCISE 1

HOW COLLEGE MAY DIFFER FROM HIGH SCHOOL

Take a few moments to jot down your ideas about how you think college will be different from your high school, in terms of the kinds of students you will be meeting, the kinds of professors you will have, the opportunities for personal and academic growth you will be exposed to, and so forth. Then use these notes as the basis for a paper of at least three pages. Bring the paper to class and, in small groups, have students read their papers to one another. When everyone in the group has heard all the papers, arrive at some agreement as to how the group believes college will be different, and report these findings to the rest of the class.

EXERCISE 2

WHAT I LIKED ABOUT HIGH SCHOOL

Write about the things you liked most about high school. Next, write about the things you liked the least. How do you hope college will be different (or the same)? Once you have completed this paper, ask your instructor whether your hopes are realistic for the college you have chosen, or use this as the basis for a discussion in the classroom.

EXERCISE 3

COMPUTING A GRADE-POINT AVERAGE

See if you can compute the GPA (GPR) for this student. Here is his grade report for the first semester:

COURSE	CREDITS	GRADE	GRADE POINTS
ENGLISH 101	3	B	
HISTORY 110	3	C+	
PSYCHOLOGY 101	3	A	
BIOLOGY 104	4	B	
UNIVERSITY 101	3	S	

To compute the number of grade points, multiply the number of credits by the value of the grade (A is 4, B is 3, C is 2, etc. A C+ would be a 2.5). Note that the grade of S, or satisfactory, does not compute into the GPA, although the credits count for graduation. A limited number of courses at your institution may be offered for satisfactory/unsatisfactory (also known as pass/fail) credit. Normally, only free electives may be taken in this manner.

1. What are the total grade points earned for the semester?

2. What are the total number of credits earned?

3. What is the GPA? *Hint:* Do not include the three credits for the S grade when you divide to determine the GPA. The correct answers are: 1. 40.5 grade points. 2. 16 credits. 3. 3.11 GPA (40.5 divided by 13).

STEP 4

JOIN A GROUP. DISCOVER WHO YOU ARE AND WHO THEY ARE.

One of the most difficult and important lessons in life involves learning to get along with others whose views, attitudes, and values may be far different from our own. Over the years, we have discovered that college provides one of the best opportunities for learning this lesson. Since people are essentially social animals, most of us have learned to make allowances for these differences in our daily relationships with others. In one sense, life could be more manageable for us all if we were more like one another. In another sense, think of what a dull world that would be! If you doubt our word, spend some time reading George Orwell's vision of the future, *1984*, which was written back in the late 1940s. In his future world, the rights of the individual have ceased to exist and everyone looks, dresses, and acts alike. Fine and dandy for the government, but absolutely depressing for humanity.

But 1984 has come and gone, and, thankfully, we still assert our individuality at every opportunity. The things you may hold dear (hard work, a good relationship with a few close friends, perhaps), may clash with those things your friends cherish (rest and relaxation, a large assortment of friends). The question is not who is right and who is wrong, for everyone is entitled to his or her own values. But by understanding another's value system, you are in a better position to understand that person, communicate with him or her, and decide whether or not you want that person for a friend. In college, because students will be arriving from many different

cherish values that may be very different from yours. We also hope you will be able to compare your values with your behaviors and determine whether the latter are consistent with the former. If not, you may wish to consider changing your behaviors or your values.

■ APPRECIATING YOURSELF

Once you feel confident about your values, you can begin to discover new ways of appreciating who you are, and not who you wish you might have been. If you're like most people, we'll bet you find it almost impossible to pay yourself a compliment. And that's a shame, because each of us needs to feel good about ourselves before we can develop meaningful relationships with others. After all, who wants to be friendly with a person who has a low opinion of him- or herself? So right now, before you read any further, take pen and paper and follow the instructions below.

■ EXERCISE 1

THE STRENGTHS EXERCISE

Put your name in bold letters across the top of your paper. Next, write the words, "My Strengths," and under that, make a list of the things about yourself you really like. Don't omit anything, no matter how trivial it may seem. Your list might include such entries as "like people," "honest to a fault," "play piano well," "tolerant of others," and so forth. For the authors of this book, one of our lists would include "shaker and mover" while the other list would include "good writer." Once you have made your list, hang it in a place where you will see it daily, and start emphasizing your strengths, not your weaknesses. In other words, instead of complaining about what you're *not* good at, start appreciating what you do so well! With this sort of positive outlook, you're ready to make some lasting relationships.

■ THE PURPOSE OF RELATIONSHIPS

Although most of us don't develop relationships to increase our life spans or to improve our minds and bodies, such improvements are side effects of a good relationship with another human being. The reasons we seek others are many, but they primarily revolve around the need to feel love, gain companionship, or simply to have fun. Mutual interests can be a basis for new relationships. A good way to find new friends is to get busy doing things you love to do. At college, this suggests you should join those organizations in which you have an interest. It is almost inevitable you will find others there who share that interest, and who probably have value systems similar, but not identical, to yours. We know from research that freshmen who join groups are also more likely to stay in college and enjoy success.

What are the advantages of a good relationship? For one thing, such a relationship underscores that you are both appreciated and re-spected, not only for your abilities, but also for yourself. A relation-ship serves as a support system, allowing you to develop your full potential as a person. What's even more wonderful is that when you tell friends about *their* strengths (what attracted you to them in the first place), they feel better about themselves and will be more willing to tell you what they like about you, too, which will make you feel even better about yourself. Finally, relationships come in many forms and guises. Don't limit yourself to too few. Other students, professors, and advisors can all serve as significant people in your lives while you are in college, and each of these individuals can help you in a unique way. Again, research tells us that freshmen who develop relationships with faculty and advisors are more likely to become sophomores!

But simply talking about values, appreciating yourself, and having positive relationships with others can't begin to explain just how essential these things are in life. So before you leave this subject, we ask that you participate in a number of exercises designed to help you clarify your own values, and to be more accepting of the values of others. Once you and your group have worked through these exercises, you should find you have more positive feelings about yourself as well as a greater understanding of where others "are coming from," and this, in turn, should give you more faith in the courage of your convictions.

■ EXERCISE 2
HOW YOU DEVELOPED YOUR VALUES

In a brief essay, and in your own words, tell how you developed your values. We suggest that you organize this paper by first exploring the sources of those values. Did you learn some of them from special friends? Did others grow out of family relationships, significant events in your life—a book you once read, a movie you saw, a trip to another part of the country or the world? Or from experiences related to church or school? You should reveal those values to the reader and tell why they are important to you, i.e., why you value them so much. Your goal in this paper should be not only to explain to others who you are, but to gain a clearer picture of yourself for you.

■ EXERCISE 3
A VALUES-BASED INTERVIEW

Find someone in your class or elsewhere on campus whom you would like to know better. Interview this person about some aspect of his or her life and about his or her ideas regarding college. Ask this person to tell you which things are important to him or her in life and which are not. You might refer to Exercise 2 above and follow the same general suggestions for this interview as you did when you were interviewing yourself. Try to write out your questions before you interview your subject, and avoid questions that can be answered "yes" or "no." (In Step Five, there is another interview assignment in which we offer additional advice on the subject of interviewing.) Once you have written the paper and perhaps shared it with others in your class, be certain you also share it with the person you have written about. Then ask that

person to tell you how accurately you have depicted him or her in
your paper. If you are doing this as a class exercise, listen carefully
to the reports others make about people you may not know. You
may find someone you'd like to meet!

■ EXERCISE 4

ANOTHER WAY OF DECLARING
YOUR VALUES

One way in which we develop into unique human beings is by
finding others we admire and attempting to be like them. Of
course, we can never be exactly like someone else, or we would
cease to be ourselves. Still, these so-called "role models" provide
us with deeds and values to which we can aspire. Role models show
us that our dreams can be achieved in part by emulating the
behaviors of others we respect.

For this exercise, think of a person you admire. This person could
be a famous person you have never met, or a member of your
family, a teacher, a special friend, or almost anybody. Either write
about the special qualities of this person, or share those qualities in
a small-group discussion to help others begin to understand you
better. Once you have done this, think of one sentence which
describes how you would like people to remember you after you
have died. Once more, either explain your choice of words
in writing, or share your phrase and the reasons behind it
in a small-group discussion. What did you learn about yourself?
About the others in the group? What do you think they learned
about you?

■ EXERCISE 5

THE CHOICE

We give special thanks to Mary Stuart Hunter of the University 101
program at USC for providing this exercise. It is best done in small

groups, but can also be done individually. If done in groups, each person should first make his or her own decisions, then share them with others in the group. The group should subsequently attempt to arrive at some consensus on its decision, and each group in the class should then share its decisions with the other groups and explain the reasons behind them. Once more, we stress that there is no one right answer in any values exercise. The important thing is to respect the opinions of another and to attempt to find some way in which you can effectively reach some sensible agreement through a give-and-take process.

The Problem

A philanthropist has offered to pay for the college education of three students from an urban ghetto area. Your committee has the task of awarding the scholarships. Eight students have been referred to your committee as possible recipients of the scholarships, and it is up to you to make the decision as to which of them will be given the opportunity to continue their education. Comments from the short essays on their application forms appear below. Please note that the philanthropist will provide funds for only three of these students, and that none of these students will be able to attend college without this scholarship.

The Students

SUZANNE "I'm an unwed mother of a 2-year-old boy. My son's father disappeared three months before Joshua was born. I still live with my parents, but things are not good at home. I think they hate the baby. I am 17 years old and work part-time at McDonald's after school to pay for day care. I am really interested in the secretarial science curriculum in college so I can get a better job and support myself and my son."

JUAN "Two years ago I left my family in Nicaragua and came to the United States for a better life. I live with grandparents who are old and sick. They keep telling me that I can make it in America, but it is so hard and I miss my mama and dad and my brothers and sisters. I've learned English pretty good but I still don't read too good. My teacher said I will graduate but I will be at the bottom of the class. I am not sure what that means. I want very much to be a success and will work hard."

DARLENE "I am 17 years old, and people tell me I'm attractive and smart. My leukemia has recently gone into remission. I want to study health education and work directly with other cancer patients. My parents have been very supportive emotionally during my illness, which has strengthened the bonds in our family. They want me to go to college, but the medical bills have taken all my college savings. Your scholarship will make a great difference in my life."

LEO "I spent the last five years in the county reform school. They said my juvenile record was really long. Now I am determined to make a new start. I am doing good in school but my buddies say that the real money can be made through drugs in the streets. I wonder if education is worth the hassle. My friends think I'm crazy to spend so much time reading, but I think I could improve myself with a college education and would work hard if accepted."

SAM "Everybody is always getting me to play basketball in the neighborhood. I'm on my high school team. I can slam dunk any way you'd like to see it, but I'm not the best player on the team so I don't think I can get an athletic scholarship. Last year, Coach told me the way to the NBA was through college, so I started studying. It's tough, but I'm trying."

SANDRA "My aunt is raising me and my three brothers. She says I'm talented in art. I like art, but the other academic subjects in school are pretty boring to me. My boyfriend is pressuring me to get married and start a family, but I dream of making it big with my paintings. I work nights as an usher at the Metropolitan Opera House. All the people I work with tell me to go to college. I think they are probably right."

PHOEBE "I'm 57 years old, and I am working on my GED at night. I have four children that I put through college working at the toll booth on the turnpike. My husband died two years ago and left me no money to live on. I like school a lot, and I make high grades. It would be a marvelous opportunity for me."

TONY "My brother wants me to join his gang, the Street Fighters, but I don't really like his friends. I do pretty well in high school and really like my sociology class. I spend a lot of time at the community center, helping the director run the place, and that's fun. I have no family life to speak of. My mom is an alcoholic, and Dad left five years ago. I want very much to get away from home and want the chance to go to college."

Your committee must choose the three recipients. It's your choice. Only you can decide. Be prepared to explain your choices.

1. _____

2. _____

3. _____

STEP 5

REALIZE THAT PROFESSORS ARE PEOPLE WHO ONCE WERE FRESHMEN, TOO

"You don't talk like a professor," the student exclaims. "You sound like real people."

Another student comments: "Professors really know what they're talking about. It's just that they don't always know how to teach it to their students." She compares this awkwardness to her high school teachers who "may not have known all there was to know, but sure knew how to say it clearly."

And that, in a nutshell, is why students and professors often have problems relating to one another. Professors are assumed to be intelligent, yet some of the things they do in class make you wonder. They rush through pages of notes, give far too many quizzes, expect too much from students. They don't care if it's homecoming weekend or Greek rush week. They expect you to be in class, to be on time, and to be current in your assignments.

Surely such creatures can't be human. Surely they can't care about your well-being. And surely they must be doing everything in their power to make you flunk their courses.

If you believe all that, you are hereby found guilty of making a generalization of the highest order. In reality, you will probably find far more professors who care about you than those who act as if you didn't exist.

What you must always remember is that establishing a positive relationship with your college professors can have a major positive impact on your life.

■ PROFESSORS ARE FORMER FRESHMEN

Many of your professors were once in the same situation in which you find yourself today—uncertain, confused, perhaps lost, and wondering where to turn for help. Your college professors are probably teaching because they love what they are doing and sense that their mission is to train the leaders of tomorrow in their disciplines. So to get to know them better, the first thing you should do is make an appointment to discuss your progress. When you reach your professor's office, look around. The walls and book-shelves and desktops will tell you a great deal about this person that you would never learn in the classroom. Professors are usually well read; some have special interests outside of their fields—such as theatre, music, sports, fitness, camping—and you may find evidence of such things in their offices. Others may speak of travels abroad or to other parts of the U.S., where they have lived, taught, or attended college. If you haven't traveled much, you can learn a great deal about faraway places and peoples from your professors.

■ WHY DO PROFESSORS TEACH?

Your college professors are probably teaching because they love their fields of study and enjoy teaching what they know to others. They certainly did not choose teaching for the money! Do they understand how you're feeling as a freshman? Perhaps not, but don't forget that every one of your professors was once a freshman, too. Chances are they will relate to your situation if you give them half a chance.

In high school, your teachers filled you with knowledge accumulated by others. Their task was to pass it on to you. Although your college teachers are also interested in passing on such knowledge as well, many of them feel the need to create new knowledge of their own, and will probably talk to you about research they are doing, professional visits they have undertaken, or recent developments in their field they have been made aware of. What's more, you will probably soon realize that while there were definite answers in high school to your questions, the same isn't always true in college. Instead of looking at issues as if they were either totally right or completely wrong, your college professors will attempt to help you see various points of view, some partially right, some partially wrong. Don't be frustrated or confused. They're merely attempting to educate you to the fact that, in reality, there are no simple answers such as you might find in a textbook. In college, we refer to this as developing a tolerance for ambiguity, a skill that will stand you in good stead for the more complex and ambiguous situations that lie in wait for you in years to come.

■ THEY WEREN'T TRAINED TO TEACH

No wonder your college professors often seem to wander from the subject, stop and check their notes to see where they are, or don't always seem to be as clear as you think they should be. Instead of taking courses which teach how to teach, they invested their energies in courses in their own academic disciplines or worked in professional organizations prior to embarking on a teaching career. You'll find lawyers teaching law, physicians teaching medicine, and corporation executives teaching management. In fact, one author of this book is a former advertising copywriter who now teaches that skill to students.

■ HOW ELSE DO PROFESSORS DIFFER FROM HIGH SCHOOL TEACHERS?

Your high school teachers probably checked your notebooks to see that they were neat, took attendance, and checked to make certain you were doing your work. In college, many professors never take roll. They won't check your notes, either, and the only clue you'll receive about the quality of your work is the grade on the paper after your professor has reviewed it. It isn't that they don't care whether you come to class or do your work. They care very much. But they also feel that you should be treated as an adult at this stage in your life.

To college professors, a real education is more than a means of getting a degree and a job. For what really distinguishes the college graduate from others is a comprehensive education in the liberal arts and sciences, which are the foundation of all knowledge. If you understand that your professors are just as interested in making you a well-rounded, educated person as they are in teaching you a specific set of facts, you will not only appreciate their efforts more, but you'll also learn to appreciate learning for its own sake.

Many college professors will take a personal interest in you. But they won't always ask you to come and see them; you will have to make the first move. Once you do, you should find that most professors appreciate a visit from students who want to talk about class. You don't have to be a genius to spend a few moments chatting with a professor. All you have to do is show a genuine interest in education. If you ask about their academic specialty, they'll be only too happy to discuss this subject with you. Try it, and you will quickly learn that this type of one-on-one interaction is an excellent opportunity to develop your knowledge beyond the classroom. Professors are required to keep office hours, and that's the time to make an appointment to see them. Don't feel as if you're bothering them; it's part of their job to make time for you. This is one of the many differences from high school, where the concept of office hours didn't exist. Furthermore, you don't lose status with your friends if you are seen talking with a professor. In college, it's the thing to do.

■ WHAT DO COLLEGE PROFESSORS DO?

A businessman once asked his college professor friend, "If you only teach 12 or 15 hours a week, what do you do the rest of the time? Sleep?" One of the most common myths about college professors is that they lead easy lives of quiet contemplation. The truth is that only physicians work longer hours than college professors, who generally put in 60 to 80 hours a week. What, then, do they do with all that other time? For one thing, they read, since it is important that they remain current in their field. This leads to additional time spent revising lecture notes. It takes far longer to prepare notes than to deliver them in class.

Professors may spend time conducting experiments, reviewing manuscripts, and writing articles, books, or speeches. They are often called upon to speak to local, regional, and national groups. They may do consulting for private corporations and government agencies for additional money. They may be writing music or plays, or creating paintings or sculptures.

When they're not doing any of these things, you will probably find them advising students. Many professors spend considerable time helping students plan their academic programs, reach career decisions, deal with personal problems, and find ways to improve their performance in the classroom.

With the time that's left, professors are asked to perform administrative duties in their colleges or units, serve on academic committees, or become involved in special college or university projects. Even when they're at home, professors are still working: grading papers and projects, preparing for tomorrow's classes. To accept this sort of schedule willingly, they must feel very strongly about the importance of the college experience.

Another thing you should remember is that many professors also happen to be wives or husbands, parents, even grandparents, and have family lives much like yours. If they're young and single, they probably date, enjoy concerts and dining out, and love to get away for vacations. You may find it difficult to believe, but your professor does have a life beyond the classroom!

■ MAKING THE MOST OF THE STUDENT-PROFESSOR RELATIONSHIP

If you remember that professors are people who respond positively to the same things as other people—politeness, consideration, tact, smiles, attention, compliments, affection, and praise—you can easily cause your professors to think more positively about you.

First, attend class regularly, and be on time. Because many students are lax in this respect, your outstanding behavior will be noticed and appreciated. Take advantage of office hours and see professors when appropriate. Rather than walk in unannounced, ask for an appointment at the end of class. Realize that professors are not people to be avoided at all costs, and that you will not be criticized by friends if you're seen with them. If you are, remember that it's their loss and your gain.

How else can you establish rapport with your professors? Come to class looking reasonably clean and well groomed. Read the assigned material before class and be prepared to ask questions, but not to the point of annoyance or distraction. Show interest in the subject. If you're having a problem developing interest in the class, or don't understand the underlying principles involved, make a beeline for your professor's office and share your concerns with him or her.

Sit near the front of the class. A number of studies have indicated that students who do so tend to make better grades. Never talk or whisper while professors are lecturing. To them, this suggests you don't care about learning anything in this class.

Finally, don't hand your professors a lot of "bull." They've been hearing this drivel for years, and can spot phony excuses a mile away. If you're sincere and have honest reasons for missing class or assignments, they are much more likely to respect you for it, and may even bend the rules about late work and grade penalties. In most cases, honesty is still the best policy.

■ ACADEMIC FREEDOM

Academic freedom is a condition and a right most college faculty enjoy at the majority of private and state supported institutions. Simply put, it is the freedom to pursue intellectual inquiry and research, or to raise questions that are legitimately related to scholarly interests and professions. Academic freedom, therefore, allows professors to raise controversial issues without risk of losing their jobs. It doesn't give them total immunity from outside pressures, but it does allow them more freedom than teachers you knew in high school.

Academic freedom is a long-established tradition in American higher education and has its origins in the development of intellectual history, dating back to the Middle Ages. Colleges and universities have found it desirable to promote the advancement of research and knowledge by giving their scholars and professors virtually unlimited freedom of inquiry, as long as human lives, rights, and privacy are not violated. This same assurance of freedom from political intervention and pressure is one of the appealing things about teaching in college. It allows a professor to enjoy a personal and intellectual freedom not possible in many other professions, and opens the doors to new ideas.

Such ideas may surprise and even anger you at times. Your professors may occasionally express some ideas and opinions that offend you. You won't like them because they'll be contrary to some of your basic values and beliefs. Professors may insult a politician you admire (the President, the governor), may speak with sarcasm about cherished institutions, and may even take a few snipes at organized religion.

Sometimes, they may be doing this just to get a reaction from you. They may believe that, in order to get you to think, they must disrupt and provoke you out of your "intellectual complacency." On the other hand, your professors may actually believe those statements you find outrageous. You will need to realize that professors are highly independent, intellectually and personally, compared to the average American. Since college professors may be free-thinkers, you may hear ideas from them that are at variance with many conventions of society. This does not mean you must agree with them in order to get good grades! It does mean, however, that you must understand such views, examine them rationally, and be prepared to defend your views if you still believe you are correct.

■ TENURE

This notion of academic freedom is related to something called "tenure." Tenure is the award a college or university gives to professors that promises them lifetime employment once they reach a certain point in their professional development. While untenured faculty also have academic freedom, tenured faculty theoretically have more of it. Tenure means that a professor may not be terminated except for extraordinary situations. These would include an act of moral turpitude, insubordination, incompetence, or a bona fide reduction in staff due to financial hardships.

■ RANK

Not all professors are "professors." In ascending order, the individual teaching you may be an instructor, lecturer, assistant professor, associate professor, or full professor. Most colleges have probationary periods of employment for faculty that they must complete before applying for promotion to the next highest rank. Promotion from assistant to associate professor may also include the award of tenure. Full professors generally teach fewer classes, have fewer students, and are more likely to be working with graduate students.

■ GRADES ARE IMPORTANT, BUT LEARNING IS MORE IMPORTANT

While it's difficult to generalize about professors, since they come in many shapes, sizes, and personalities, it's relatively safe to assume that most of them believe in the value of a liberal arts education.

Perhaps you have heard that a liberal arts education is important because more and more employers are seeking individuals with the analytical and communications skills such an education provides. To a professor, the value of such an education goes far beyond that. The word *liberal*, from the Latin *libero*, means "free." The goal of a liberal arts education is to free your mind from the biases, superstitions, prejudices, and lack of knowledge that characterizes many people who fail to benefit from such an education.

To free you of such restraints, it may be necessary to provoke, challenge, and disturb you by presenting you with new ideas, beliefs, and values that may differ from your previous perceptions. In college, as in life, you will have to learn to tolerate—if not accept—opinions that are vastly different from yours. You need not always accept those opinions, but you should learn to evaluate them for yourself instead of basing your responses on what others have always told you.

Most college professors believe freshmen are woefully underprepared to do college work, many through no fault of their own. As a result, they'll challenge you to raise your standards to theirs, instead of lowering theirs to meet yours. Don't be surprised, therefore, if your grades aren't as high as they were in high school. This may also mean that you will have to spend much more time studying to make the same grades you made in high school. College professors tend to reserve A's for the very few at the top of the class who have done superior work. Some professors will not award any A's in a given semester if they feel the work was not up to their standards for this high grade.

Two things need to be said about grades at this point. First, the only reason for grades is that they document your proficiency in a class. Far more important than the difference between an A and a B is how much you have learned—how much intellectual growth has taken place. Far too many students believe that a high grade-point average is all it takes to be well educated and successful in life. To the contrary, many individuals whose grades were in the middle range in college are among the most successful of their generation. High grades won't hurt you; they simply are no guarantee of future success. If you study properly, and develop a genuine interest in class material, you will generally find that high grades will follow. Our advice is, don't work for the high grades; work instead to understand and appreciate and find meaning in the content of the course.

■ WHAT PROFESSORS WANT FROM
THEIR STUDENTS

Good professors frequently have students approach them at the end of the term to tell them how much they enjoyed the class. Professors may appreciate this, but what they would much rather hear is, "I learned a lot from you this semester and I just wanted to express my appreciation." Enjoyment should result from the positive learning experience; it shouldn't result from enjoyment for its own sake. Remember, your professors are not primarily entertainers. If they entertain out of proportion to teaching, they may be shortchanging you in the long run.

Much has been written about professors who don't really care about students, but are interested only in teaching them new ideas. It's difficult to see how these two thoughts are consistent with one another, for some level of caring must exist before learning can be passed from one individual to another. If you doubt that your professors care, ask them. The answer may be revealing to both of you.

Finally, remember that professors will like you more, even though they may not show it, if you participate in class discussions, complete your assignments on time, ask questions during class, make appointments to see them, comment on lecture materials, or simply smile and say "hello" when you meet them on campus.

During the remainder of your life, you'll meet many interesting individuals. Few will be more complex than your college professors. One or two of your college faculty may have a significant effect on your life. For this reason alone, it pays to know them well during your college years.

EXERCISE 1

INTERVIEWING A PROFESSOR

Choose one of your current professors and interview him or her. To do this, you should arrange in advance for an appointment of at least thirty minutes, preferably in your professor's office. When you arrive, have pen and paper ready, along with a general outline of topics you will be covering. Your goal is to find out why the professor chose his or her present academic discipline, what other teaching or professional experience he or she has had, how he or she would describe the ideal student and the ideal teacher, what his or her principles of good teaching consist of, and what he or she expects of students. Write the paper as if it were a portrait, in words, of this person. Do not simply list facts! If this is part of a class exercise, share your comments with others in the class. What might such an exercise accomplish for you? For the professor you interviewed? For others in your class? Can you describe any difference in your relationship with this professor as a result of the interview? If there is a difference, what have you learned from this experience?

JOURNEY THREE

DISCOVERING WHAT A FRESHMAN NEEDS TO KNOW MOST

Up to this point, we have been working to put you at ease about the exciting years of college that lie ahead for you. To review, first we discussed the value of attending college. Next, we talked about the differences between college and high school, and focused on two of the most significant relationships you will have in college: other students and your professors. Having done all this, we assume you're ready for the next journey—and it's a very important one, as you can tell from the title! What do freshmen need to know most? Our years of experience in working with freshmen have led us to believe that, although individuals have varying needs, almost all freshmen need the three commodities we're about to spring on you: help in writing effectively, an understanding of college terminology, and an exploration of resources on your campus that can enrich your college experience far beyond the classroom. Together with the fourth journey, this is by far the most significant part of your orientation to college. Read carefully, read thoroughly, and follow through with the exercises. We promise that they can make a difference!

STEP 6

WRITING EFFECTIVELY.
THE KEY TO DISCOVERY.

This journey begins with a discussion of writing because it is the critical skill that can open hidden doors in your mind and other doors on campus and beyond. Plain and simple, if you have problems writing, you're going to have problems learning. If you don't learn, you're going to miss out on much of what college has to offer. For one reason or another, the majority of entering college freshmen approach writing as if it were a task they wish they could avoid, and their writing suffers because of this attitude. We won't attempt to place the blame on teachers in the public schools, because that may not be fair. We do know, however, that most young people have hangups about writing because they were taught that rules of grammar, punctuation, spelling, organization, capitalization, etc., etc., were more important than the content of their writing. We're going to dispute that argument in this step, so be forewarned that you may be asked to temporarily forget old ideas and consider some totally new ones. But as we said earlier, that's what learning is all about.

Before you can write with authority, you need permission to do so. That's a simple statement, but hidden within it is the reason many high school and college students encounter grave problems when asked to write a paper.

Students write poorly because they don't understand what writing really is. So first, you must understand that writing is a process by which we set down thoughts. Writing is also, and more importantly, a process through which we *create new thoughts*. And not so incidentally, it's a darned good way to set down those thoughts for posterity so that others can read them, think about them, and, if they care enough, act on them.

The reason many students become so hung up on writing is that for years we've been stressing all the wrong things: grammar, spelling, punctuation, syntax, organization, thesis sentences, metaphors, similes, etc. Now before you get the wrong idea, we need to add that these items are certainly not unimportant. Quite the contrary, they are practically essential for good writing. But they come much later in the process. They are, by and large, the mechanical steps one must commit to memory. The other part of writing, the thinking part, needs to be developed ahead of and independently from the mechanics. No doubt, some people can manage both at the same time, but since there's no need for such agony, why do it?

Artists tell us that the reason most of us can't draw worth a toot is that we are drawing from the wrong side of the brain, the left, or logical, side. When one uses logic as a basis for drawing, the goal is to get the thing done as efficiently as possible. So even when would-be artists are looking at a subject's eye, what they draw is not that person's eye but the generic symbol for "eye," a perfect oval with a dot in the center. To confuse the left brain, one must look intently at the model and, pretending the point of the pencil is not on the paper but actually on the eye, begin to slowly follow the real curve of the eye on the sketch pad while looking always at the real eye. This tedious maneuver should frustrate the logical brain until, bored and helpless, it turns away from the task to allow creativity to flourish.

The same approach can free writing of the dreary logic that, while necessary, tends to sap the vigor from our thoughts if we allow it to take charge too early in the game. Using this argument, we might explain that students who have writing problems are trying to do it all in one step because that is the way we have taught them to do it, and also because no one has ever made them believe they have anything significant or interesting to write about.

Here's a way around those blocks: freewriting. Freewriting is a process which allows you to forget the rules momentarily and concentrate on the thinking. To relieve you of anxiety, you need to know that your piece of writing will not be read aloud to anyone, will not be shared in any other way, will not be graded, will not be read by any instructor, etc. The only direction here is, "write." Write about anything that comes into your mind, but don't sit and look around and wait for inspiration to strike. Start writing immediately, even though you know you aren't at the beginning of a thought. Waiting for the beginning has stopped many a writer from ever getting started. Just plunge right in—now.

Ideally, you should keep this up for ten minutes. Then, if you're writing as part of a group (which is always the best way to do this), each writer should share his or her feelings about the exercise. How did it feel to write this way? Was it difficult to get started? Why? Why not? How did this differ from other writing experiences?

Next, we're going to move into "focused" freewriting, or freewriting with a topic in mind. A logical topic at this point would be, "What I do that makes it difficult (or easy) for me to write." Take another ten minutes to do this, and know that you will be asked (but not forced!) to share these thoughts with the group.

When everyone is finished with this task, several individuals should volunteer to read their papers aloud to the group. After each paper is read, others in the group should offer comments on what they heard and how that paper was the same as or different from their papers. Sharing such thoughts in a group should give writers a clearer understanding of why they find writing difficult, and they could now proceed to write a more comprehensive paper on the subject "Why many people have trouble writing effectively."

Another fascinating way to generate ideas on a given topic is through the process known as looping. Looping uses an inductive reasoning process to coax us to write about a topic freely. Instead of providing the topic and letting it go at that, looping allows writers to approach the topic from a number of different angles until, suddenly, the writers begin to see a pattern emerging which they can use in a subsequent draft of the paper.

Suppose, for example, that you were going to write a paper on apathy. Here is how you would approach it through the looping method.

First, for ten minutes, you would write your first thoughts about apathy. Remember, this gives you the freedom to plunge right into the middle of a thought if that's what you think of first.

Then, for ten more minutes, you would write about apathy in a different manner. You would begin by imagining you were in a vast art gallery and that, as you turned a corner and glanced at the tiny brass plate at the bottom of a painting, you read the title, "Apathy." In your imagination, you would look up at the painting, study it for a few moments, and then write for ten minutes on "a portrait of apathy."

Next, you would imagine that you and "apathy" were sitting comfortably on two chairs, and that you were having a dialogue, or conversation, and for these ten minutes you would be asked to write that conversation down on paper.

Following that, you would write for ten minutes on "lies about apathy," having as much fun as you cared to.

You could follow these with loops that are written from different points of view. For example, a young person's view of apathy, an elderly person's view of apathy, etc.

When you have done all this, you have lots of writing, but you certainly don't have a finished paper. The next step, then, would be to find a quiet place, and, using that great mountain of words you have just committed to paper, write a rough draft of your paper on apathy. You might even want to narrow the topic down to a certain aspect of apathy, or a comparison of apathy and enthusiasm.

You should give yourself plenty of time to complete this step. Once again, share your draft aloud in small groups, with each person reading his or her paper to the others. After each paper is read, members of the group should offer critical feedback to the writer in the form of constructive advice on what worked for them and what didn't, and how the writer might improve the piece. With the help of such advice and enthusiasm, each writer can now proceed to write a finished piece that is enriched by the input of others and provides the writer with new insight into the topic.

At this point, you will need to clean up your paper by observing the accepted rules of spelling, punctuation, and so forth.

Before we conclude, we need to stress that writing has a place in every classroom. When Gail Hearn, associate professor of biology at Beaver College, sees a bunch of blank faces staring at her in the middle of a lecture, she stops where she is and asks her students to write for five minutes about what she's just been talking about. Professor Hearn says such exercises help students become better writers and better thinkers. They are more likely to learn something, she maintains, when they can write about it.

Some math teachers have students keep a log in which they write down the steps they took to solve a mathematical problem. The idea is that, in the process, students will develop skills for tackling more difficult problems.

In courses with difficult readings, says Teresa J. Vilardi of Bard College, students can be encouraged to get more deeply involved with the material by writing a dialogue for characters in it.

"The main thing students need to learn is how not to do that one-night stand for writing assignments," says Peter Elbow, director of writing programs at the State University of New York at Stony Brook. Requiring students to hand in early drafts helps them see that revisions are as important as other assignments, he says. Elbow is also the author of two books which discuss this writing movement in detail: *Writing Without Teachers,* and *Writing With Power.*

How else can you improve your skills as a writer?

■ REVIEW ONE ANOTHER'S WORK

By giving feedback to classmates, you can sharpen your ability to evaluate and improve your own writing. Such consultations should be in small groups and well structured. You must learn to react to a piece of writing with something more than a simple, "I liked it."

More useful are such questions as, "What did you like most about the piece?" and "What is the main idea of this paper?"

■ ASK TEACHERS TO SUPPORT YOUR ACCOMPLISHMENTS

This amounts to nothing more than having them mark the strong parts of a paper and encourage you to build on your strengths.

■ WHAT NOW?

Well, we warned you that some of the ideas about writing you were about to read might seem unconventional to you. All we ask that you do at this point, however strange the suggestions may seem, is to try them. Ideally, you should be led through the exercises by your instructor in a group setting. But if that isn't possible, you can still help yourself become a better writer by paying attention to the ideas expressed here. If you can convince three or four other students to form a writing group with you, so much the better. For now, work through the following suggested exercises and decide for yourself whether this approach to the writing process is helping you become a more confident writer.

■ EXERCISE 1

WRITING ABOUT WRITING

All through life, and especially in school, each of us has been through many writing experiences. Please think about one or two of these that either made you feel very good or very bad about your ability to write. In your essay, describe how this made you feel about your writing, and conclude by reflecting on how the information in this section on writing applies to those earlier writing experiences and how you now feel about your writing abilities.

■ EXERCISE 2

NONSTOP FREEWRITING

If you haven't already done so, write for about ten minutes on anything that comes to mind. Don't worry about spelling, grammar, punctuation, etc., at this point. Just write. If you run out of ideas, write, "I can't think of anything" until other ideas pop into your head. Then write about those ideas. At the end of ten minutes, stop and rest. Then write about how it felt to write this way. Share your thoughts with classmates.

■ EXERCISE 3

LOOPING

Practice the looping process as described in this section. Use any topic you wish. Once you have gone through at least four loops on the same topic, determine what your next step in writing a paper on this topic might be, and whether the looping process has helped you get started.

STEP 7

LEARN HOW TO SPEAK "COLLEGE"

In every field of endeavor, there is a special language, or "jargon," which is somewhat undecipherable to so-called outsiders. Higher education is no different; its special language, which may roll glibly off the tongues of professors, admissions counselors, and registrars, is often a complex gobbledegook of nonmeaning to new freshmen. To ease the trauma of learning the language of college, at the end of this book you'll find a glossary of terms we have accumulated over the years. There are no exercises at the end of this section because the entire section is an exercise in learning new words and new meanings for old words, and that is precisely what your assignment is for this step. Turn now to the glossary, beginning on p. 187, and read through it completely. If you're in a freshman orientation class or freshman seminar, test one another on the meanings of these important words.

STEP 8

LEARN WHAT'S OUT THERE FOR YOU

"Hold on a minute!" you're probably saying. "Haven't we been finding out about college throughout the first seven steps of this book? What's left to learn?"

Obviously, if we had told you all we thought you needed to know about college in seven steps, this book would have been much shorter! This step and the next are the introductions to the fourth journey, which follows, and it's a long journey, to be sure. What you will learn as you follow the path we've outlined is that a vast number of helping resources are available at many college and university campuses to help students in ways you may never have dreamed possible. We're not speaking of resources in the classroom, but of the many professionals beyond the classroom who can play an important role in your development as a young adult.

So to begin this exploration, we're simply going to list the types of resources we're talking about. Study them carefully, then follow the directions for the exercise at the end of this section.

■ ACADEMIC ADVISING

Many campuses now maintain special centers where full-time advisors are available to meet with students at any time. Do you have an academic advisor yet? If not, or if you're not getting all the help you need, find out if there is an advising center on your campus and use it.

■ ACADEMIC SKILLS

The academic skills center teaches reading and study skills, such as note taking, preparing for exams, listening, time management, test taking, etc. Typically, such a center offers short courses at little or no charge and may provide individual counseling and tutoring. It's where you learn how to learn.

■ ALCOHOL AND DRUG AWARENESS

Such centers offer programs to help you make responsible decisions regarding the use of alcoholic beverages. Illegal drugs are also discussed at many of these centers. These programs, rather than preaching to you about the evils of substance abuse, try to help you understand that the decision to drink is a personal one, and should not be determined by peer pressure. Many of the myths about drinking are also covered.

■ ANXIETY AND STRESS MANAGEMENT

Learning the basic principles of relaxation through such methods as self-hypnosis or biofeedback at counseling centers can help you become a better scholar as well as a more fulfilled individual. Knowing how to combat stress can be particularly helpful in managing test-taking anxiety.

■ ASSERTIVENESS TRAINING

Assertiveness training, also offered at counseling centers, teaches the skills of respectful and responsible interpersonal communications. Knowing how to stand up for your rights without denying the rights of others can be extremely helpful, whether you're interacting with parents, professors, or friends. Such training can be especially helpful for freshmen from small towns who find themselves at large universities.

■ CAREER PLANNING

Whether you have decided on an academic major or not, your career center may prove invaluable. In addition to its career library, where you may study hundreds of career possibilities, you may also be able to take various career inventories and receive personal one-on-one counseling, which can help you determine what types of work you enjoy most, which kinds of work you have the needed skills for, and which careers fit your preferred lifestyle.

■ CHAPLAINS

Chaplains representing major religious denominations provide personal counseling as well as worship services and fellowship for students away from home.

■ COOPERATIVE EDUCATION/STUDENT EMPLOYMENT

Cooperative education programs allow you to work one term in your major academic field, and to attend classes during alternate terms. Student employment simply means finding jobs on the campus, usually in the form of student assistantships, work-study programs, or other options.

■ COMMUTER SERVICES

If you live off-campus, the office of commuter services normally provides current listings of apartments, houses, and rooms for rent; roommate listings; babysitting lists; and other useful information.

■ COUNSELING

Most campus personal counseling centers are staffed by licensed counseling psychologists who can help students with personal and interpersonal concerns, ranging from a disagreeable roommate to prolonged periods of depression. Services generally are free, and are always confidential. Many freshman problems are *normal*. Needing and receiving counseling doesn't mean you are sick. Counseling is a growth and learning experience.

■ DISABLED STUDENT SERVICES

This office supports those students who are disabled and need help in overcoming physical, educational, or emotional barriers to achieve their full educational potential. It is also an excellent source of information on how to interact with disabled students if you feel some anxiety about this.

■ FINANCIAL AID AND SCHOLARSHIPS

Your campus financial aid office coordinates all financial assistance received by students on your campus. It administers major programs of financial aid and receives and authorizes all outside scholarships and grants. If you need financial aid, you should contact this office for information on how to apply and what is available to you.

■ GREEK AFFAIRS

If you are interested in joining a fraternity or sorority, you can contact the coordinator of Greek affairs in the student affairs division of your school.

■ HEALTH CENTERS/INFIRMARIES/HOSPITALS

We hope you won't need these facilities. All the same, you need to know they exist for your benefit. Many of these facilities include specialized clinics and medical specialists such as gynecologists, psychiatrists, orthopedic specialists, and so on. Medical personnel not only examine and treat student illnesses but also prescribe medicines, which are available at significantly reduced costs. This may also be the place to visit if you need advice on birth control.

■ HEALTH ENRICHMENT

Many campuses offer students guidance in the many areas of personal health, including nutrition, weight control, physical fitness, exercise, and sexuality.

■ HOUSING

Your campus housing office can help you locate on- or off-campus housing and advise you on the advantages and disadvantages of each. Hall advisors or dorm proctors who live in the residence halls can also help you become oriented to campus life through personal counseling and dorm-wide programs.

■ INTRAMURAL AND RECREATIONAL SPORTS

Dorms, organizations, and other campus groups may form teams and compete with one another in organized intramurals playoffs, with an emphasis on recreation and fun. You can be athletic in college even if you don't make the varsity team!

■ LAW ENFORCEMENT AND SAFETY

With responsibility for parking, vehicle registration, policing, transportation, fire safety, and crime prevention, the law enforcement and safety division also assists students through crime awareness programs that help protect your property and person.

■ LEGAL SERVICES

Your campus may or may not offer legal services to students. If a law school exists on your campus, you might want to check with them to see if upperclass students are available to you for legal counseling.

■ LIBRARY

Knowing how to use your campus library will make a significant difference in your academic performance during your four years in college. Be certain you receive a proper orientation. If one is not offered in a class, ask the reference librarian in the main library to help you. Be certain you also follow the directions in the library exercise in Step 12 of this book.

■ LEADERSHIP

Student leadership programs introduce the concept of leadership and how it is relevant to college and life. Connections are made between college and career/community leadership in programs such as this.

■ PHYSICAL EDUCATION CENTER

One of the best ways to reduce student stress is to become involved in physical sports. The campus PE center may offer such varied facilities as basketball, tennis, racketball, handball, and squash courts; a dance studio; a swimming pool; an archery range; a weight room; and many more indoor and outdoor facilities.

■ STUDENT ACTIVITIES

Clubs, organizations, fraternities and sororities, student media, and intramurals are usually administered by the student activities department. Becoming familiar with this office can help you plan your extracurricular activities.

■ STUDENT GOVERNMENT

Student government associations are often looking for students— freshmen included—who are interested in becoming involved in campus governance.

■ STUDENT MEDIA

Students interested in reporting, copyediting, layout and design, photography, feature writing, advertising sales, radio, and television, should find out about student media (newspaper, yearbook, literary magazine, radio and television stations) on campus.

■ STUDENT UNION

Your union offers cultural programs, movies, activities, as well as many other ways to fill your leisure time on campus. Find the union building and find out what it offers.

■ UNDECLARED MAJORS

If you have not chosen a major, you will probably be assigned to a center for undeclared majors, which will provide academic advice and career-planning services. It's perfectly normal not to have a declared major as a freshman, but since most schools require you to have a major before you graduate, it's important to get the help you need from this center.

■ THEATRE ON CAMPUS

You don't have to be a theatre major to enjoy the live dramatic and musical productions on campus. Most colleges offer first-rate productions at a fraction of the price you would pay downtown.

■ VOLUNTEER SERVICES

Many schools maintain offices that help you become involved with volunteer service agencies in the community. Often such work enables you to earn academic credit for certain "on the job" courses. This invaluable experience will also look good on your résumé.

■ WRITING

Most colleges maintain a writing center where you can get free assistance in improving your writing skills; in getting themes, book reviews, and term papers in proper shape, and so forth.

That's our list of resources, and we hope that you will be able to add to it when you make a thorough canvass of your campus. Remember, if you regard college as strictly classes and homework, you're not really giving it a fair chance!

EXERCISE 1

NEEDS AND RESOURCES.
MAKING A MATCH.

If you haven't already done so, make a list of your needs as a freshman. Then, attempt to find a resource on this list, or from a list in your campus directory, that fits each of those needs. If you are already on campus, use the campus telephone directory to find out how to get in touch with these services on your campus. Your instructor may wish to ask each class member to gather information on a number of these resources, and to share that information with the rest of the class. You may also want to contact representatives of some of the most popular groups to make presentations in your classroom about their services.

JOURNEY FOUR
FINDING THE ANSWERS

Although every journey and step in this book is important, this journey will be your longest and most crucial. As you make your way through the following steps, you will be learning about the critical skills you will be using in college, about the most important things you will need to know, and about using these skills and this knowledge to move closer to becoming your own person. Follow the steps carefully. Work at mastering them one step at a time, and when you complete this journey, you will be ready to take the fifth, and final one in this book, as you become responsible for determining your own personal growth.

STEP 9

HOW TO IMPROVE YOUR
STUDY SKILLS

Perhaps you are one of the rare people on this earth who just naturally knows how to study—although goodness knows where you learned this valuable skill, since it's one of those things like raising children that we are simply expected to know about. Think about it. We're sent to public school for twelve years, and many of us go to college for another four, and pay dearly for the privilege of becoming an educated person. Yet no one actually sits us down in class and says, "Here's how to study." It's no wonder we make so many blunders on this score and end up feeling so frustrated!

To promise that in the next few pages we can teach you everything you didn't learn about studying during your twelve years in school would be ridiculous. What we are going to attempt to do, however, is raise some issues about effective studying and offer you advice on where to get further help right on your own campus.

We begin with some general, but highly important suggestions. Sit as close to the instructor as you can on the first day of class. Students who sit up front tend to get better grades. The closer you sit, the fewer visual distractions you have. If your instructor has assigned seating, plead nearsightedness.

Copy down everything on the board. Any note there may hold the clue to an exam item. If it's important enough to write on the board, it may be an important issue in the course.

When you're away from the classroom, there are many things you can do to improve your study habits. Try to find a place for study and nothing else. Even if it's a corner of your room, stake it out for studying and never do anything else there. In doing so, you can condition yourself to study whenever you find yourself in that special place.

All well and good, you might be saying, but how do I make myself sit in that place and study? The answer is time management.

■ TIME MANAGEMENT

Before you can improve your study skills, you will have to learn how to make the most of your study time. A time management schedule can help you develop a weekly routine that allows you to be successful both in your college work and in your leisure activities.

How do you manage time effectively? To begin with, make a weekly chart divided into hours for each day, from 8 a.m. to 8 p.m. First, fill in those blocks that represent the classes you are taking. Then block in any scheduled meetings you will have to attend. Leave time for meals and rest, and look at the rest of the empty squares. How can you use the time immediately before a class? Perhaps you should reserve this hour for "reviewing psychology notes." What about your evening study hours? Instead of just blocking in time to "study," be specific about what you need to study and in what subject. If you train yourself to establish this weekly schedule, leaving yourself sufficient time for fun and friends, you will find it easier to balance your study hours with your leisure hours. All you need to promise yourself is that you will stick to your schedule, and that works both ways. If a friend invites you out for a movie, your answer might be, "Let's go at 9 after I finish studying." If your study time is over, be certain you get some relaxation as scheduled, too!

Another way to manage your time efficiently is to get into the habit of carrying a pocket calendar with you at all times. You can find one at the campus bookstore that has sufficient space for you to record important events (dates of exams, appointments with advisors, social events, club meetings, etc.). Your professors probably carry

EXAMPLE OF A WELL-PLANNED SCHEDULE

	MONDAY	TUESDAY	WEDNESDAY	THURSDAY	FRIDAY
8:00					
9:00	PSYCHOLOGY 101	REVIEW SOCIOLOGY NOTES	PSYCHOLOGY 101	REVIEW SOCIOLOGY NOTES	PSYCHOLOGY 101
10:00	STUDY: Reading Room (RR) PSYCHOLOGY NOTES	SOCIOLOGY 104	STUDY: Reading Room (RR) PSYCHOLOGY NOTES	SOCIOLOGY 104	STUDY: Reading Room (RR) PSYCHOLOGY NOTES
11:00	ENGLISH 102		ENGLISH 102		ENGLISH 102
12:00					
1:00	MATH 140	REVIEW HISTORY NOTES	MATH 140	REVIEW HISTORY NOTES	MATH 140
2:00	REVIEW MATH NOTES	HISTORY 114	REVIEW MATH NOTES	HISTORY 114	REVIEW MATH NOTES
3:00	← ———— BAND ————————→				
4:00	← ———— REHEARSAL ————————→				
5:00			FRATERNITY MEETING		
6:00	OUTLINE PAPER FOR ENGLISH (DUE NEXT WEEK)	WRITE DRAFT FOR ENGLISH PAPER / READ SOCIOLOGY	↓	STUDENT GOVERNMENT MEETING	
7:00				↓	
8:00	↓	↓		PROOFREAD DRAFT FOR ENGLISH PAPER	

such calendars with them so that they don't forget appointments with you. If you're uncertain as to what type of calendar to buy, you might ask a professor for advice.

Now that we've asked you to deliberately adhere to a schedule for studying and having fun, let's discuss some of your specific studying needs.

■ READING A TEXTBOOK

Don't read a textbook in the same manner as you read a book for pleasure. Experts in the field claim you should read the introduction, headings, and subtitles of a chapter before you read the main body of the chapter. If the chapter ends with a summary of its contents, you might even read this summary first. The reason for this "pre-reading" is to help you become more comfortable with the topics being covered before you have to concentrate on the details.

Now that you have read the "shell" of the chapter, begin reading the chapter itself. Each time you reach the end of a section, or a new subheading, stop and explain to yourself, in your own words, what you have just read. If you find that underlining or highlighting certain key phrases helps you remember them, that's fine. But we suggest that you read several paragraphs *before* you attempt to underline or highlight. If you don't, you may find yourself marking too many words and phrases instead of only the most significant ones.

Does the chapter you're reading have graphs, charts, or diagrams? If so, they're obviously there for a reason, and it may be worth your while to stop and study them when you have completed the portion of the text referring to them. Finally, after you have read a complete chapter, try to explain, in your own words how the ideas in the chapter were organized and look for relationships between ideas. Jotting down these relationships may prove invaluable when you are listening to the next class lecture. They may also provide you with a wealth of information for participating in class discussion or raising questions, two additional ways to remember the material covered.

The professionals at study skills centers offer these other bits of useful advice: If you find yourself reading the same line over and over, place an index card over the preceding line to break yourself of the habit. If you find yourself saying every word of the text aloud (which can slow you down greatly), place a pencil between your lips. If you talk, the pencil will drop. Try it, and see if it works for you.

■ LECTURE NOTES

Classroom lectures are critical to the learning process. If they were not, you could simply buy your textbooks and do all of your studying at home. That isn't the way we learn best, however. Lectures should be designed to amplify your readings, to explain a central idea, or to give you the oppportunity for a greater understanding of the subject through interaction with people who are experts in their fields: your professors. Your professors also designed their notes to tell you what they feel are the most important points in the lesson. Lecture notes, therefore, can be extremely important. If you want to have lecture notes that make sense and will help you learn, the first rule is to read the assignment *before* it is discussed in lecture. Familiarizing yourself with the material in advance will help you see how your professor is "filling in the blanks" that may have been left by your textbook author. Many professors, rather than simply rehash information you were to have read in your text, will provide interesting sidelights to the textual information. If you haven't done your reading in advance, you may be totally lost.

One way to organize your notes, especially if your professor tends to be rather disorganized, is to leave a wide margin on one side of the page, separated from the rest of the page by a vertical line. As you take notes, write a major topic to the left of the line (in the margin) and take notes pertaining to that topic on the right. When the professor switches to a new topic, write that topic under the first, and take notes opposite. Should he or she return to the previous topic, you should have left room so that you can now add information in the proper space. Most importantly, as soon as you can get to it, you should review and rewrite your notes, filling in what you may not have had time to write. The sooner you do this, the more you will recall the essence of what the professor has been saying. Waiting to review notes just prior to an exam can be futile indeed.

Speaking of reviewing for an exam—even though you have rewritten your notes after class, make a point of reviewing them prior to the next class. Doing this regularly will help you see the connections between topics discussed previously and topics your professor is currently discussing. Another valuable suggestion for exams is to review your lecture notes and text with the goal of creating questions from the material that might be on the exam. Chances are you will be fairly accurate in predicting the questions to be asked. Now all you need to do is write out the answers and you will be in good shape for the real thing!

In a broader sense, the quality of your notes can depend to a great degree on your attitude in the classroom. Don't slouch; it will cause you to miss many of the important points of a lecture. Concentrate on the lecturer, not on the crack in the ceiling. Force yourself to become so involved with the lecture that you are aware of nothing else. It's only for an hour or so, and your purpose in being there is to learn. Remember, even dull subjects become interesting once you are involved.

Finally, raise questions in class at the appropriate time. A good question helps you relate one idea to another, and helps fix those ideas in your mind. Never feel you are asking a stupid question; the fact that you are asking something is a sign that you are interested, and your professor will appreciate that interest.

Taking good notes may be your single most critical study skill. It was for one of your authors, who had problems with exams until he learned how to take good notes. Once he learned this skill, he could "ace" virtually any exam. Perhaps you will be able to do this, too!

■ REMEMBERING MATERIAL

Most of us think we have poor memories when, in actuality, we are probably trying to memorize by repetition, which usually provides us with few clues as to the meaning of ideas or of their importance. What you need to be doing instead is working on a system of memorization that has some meaning beyond mere remembrance of meaningless phrases. For example, grouping information that is related is one way to remember it. If you can remember the key word that relates to all topics in a group, you will have an easier time remembering the details, too. Another way to remember meaningful information is to explain the material, not in the words of your professor or textbook author, but in your own words. Reviewing text and lecture information on a weekly basis will also make the memorization process easier and more natural.

■ PREPARING FOR A TEST

When you take an examination, do the easy questions first. But take your time! When you have finished, be sure you recheck the "easy" answers as well as the difficult ones. In your haste to do the easy ones first, you may have made some careless mistakes which can cost you precious points on your final score. On an essay test, write something down for every item. You can only get a zero if you leave an item blank. But if you write something, even though it may not be the best answer, you may score a few points for your efforts.

Be neat on an essay test. A paper that is easy to read tends to get a higher grade than a sloppy one which causes the scorer problems as he or she tries to decipher every other word. By the same token, a typed term paper tends to get a higher grade than one written by hand.

On an objective test, if you change your mind, change your answer. Many studies have proven that you can expect to pick up more points than you will lose by changing answers. Just be certain your gut feelings are right!

Some educators suggest you study your easiest subjects first. This can help relax you and prepare you for the more difficult tasks ahead. Others stress that understanding the material will get you far higher marks than simply memorizing without understanding. Your professors will be able to tell if you are merely playing their own words back and haven't the slightest idea what they mean. If you don't understand, ask questions in class.

Prior to exams, ask professors to tell you the type of exam they will be giving. This can be of great help to you in preparing. While taking exams, don't be afraid to ask your professors for help in defining a question if it isn't clear to you. Let them decide whether or not they can provide you with such help.

■ WRITING EXAMINATIONS

Before you answer the first question, read all the questions and choose the items that appear to be the easiest for you. Next do the ones that seem somewhat more difficult, and save the most difficult for last. Not only will you be able to answer more items, you may even gain confidence by the time you reach the most difficult questions.

Be certain you read directions carefully and that you answer only as many items as directed. If you don't choose the options the professor gives you, he or she has every right to take only the first questions you have answered.

Be direct, use proper English, and answer only what is asked. If you pad your answers, you may be displaying your ignorance. Make certain you answer each part of every question, however.

If time is running out, and you are unable to complete the details of a question but know the procedure, it may be worthwhile to outline the procedure you would follow if you had the time. You may earn some points for this effort.

Use all the time allowed. If you finish early, spend the remaining time checking your answers. The best students generally finish last, not first! Write clearly, using a dark pen (not a light pencil). If your paper is hard to read, you will probably lose points.

Above all, get enough rest the night before and come to class refreshed and prepared. If you study properly and feel rested, you will have more confidence in your ability to do well. Avoid drugs that keep you awake. Besides being dangerous, they tend to cloud your thinking and rarely prove helpful.

If you are having trouble managing your time or studying, ask about the services offered by the study skills center on your campus. Don't let things deteriorate until there's little or no chance of your catching up for the semester.

We realize you may not be able to employ all of these study techniques. All we ask is that you make some effort to use those that seem appropriate, and measure their value by the changes you see, not only in your grades, but in your enhanced interest in your classes.

EXERCISE 1
CHOOSING STUDY METHODS

Practice at least five of the suggestions offered in this chapter for a week. At the end of the week, write an essay in which you discuss how effective each of these methods was for you.

EXERCISE 2
GROUP SHARING OF STUDY METHODS

If you are using this book in a class, suggest that class members form small groups. Each group should be responsible for exchanging study ideas for a particular area, such as studying for tests, reading textbooks, writing essay exams, answering objective exams, classroom participation and its effect on grades and learning, etc. A recorder in each group should make note of the suggestions offered, and each group should then share its suggestions with the other groups.

STEP 10

YOUR ACADEMIC ADVISOR, THE PERSON WITH THE ANSWERS.

"I can't get along with my history professor, and he's the only one teaching the class I need. What should I do? Is the course required?"

"Hey, why do I have to take a course in Western civilization for a degree in journalism?"

"Okay, now that you've signed my advisement form, what next?"

"I still don't understand why you won't let me take this course for degree credit."

"I'm a freshman and I don't understand what you mean by my grade-point average."

"I'm graduating this spring, and I'm scared to death I won't be able to find a job."

"I don't think I'm in the right major and I don't know what to do about it."

"My grades are going to be terrible this semester. Will I be suspended?"

"I just broke up with my girl and I can't concentrate on my class work, and there's a big exam next week in my physics class."

"I know this sounds stupid, but I'm so depressed I can't think, and I don't even know why."

It would take a wizard to come up with the perfect answers for all of these questions, and you don't find many wizards hanging around these days. But the next best person to answer such requests is probably the man or woman who has been assigned to be your academic advisor during your years in college.

Who is this person, and why is he or she willing to take so much time to listen to your questions? Most likely, your academic advisor is either a professor on the faculty of your academic major or a professional advisor who is employed by your college or department to do nothing but assist students with academic needs.

Academic needs? Hold on; lots of those questions we just posed aren't really about academic needs. Or are they? That's another question your academic advisor will have to answer, but we'll make an attempt right here. Because every one of those questions involves a problem that has some bearing on the academic performance of a student, they certainly are within the purview of academic advising. Granted, not all advisors are trained counselors or psychotherapists, but if they're worth their salt, they're empathetic individuals who genuinely care about your well-being and know where to send you on campus if they can't provide all the help you need.

■ MISCONCEPTIONS ABOUT ADVISING

Both faculty and students share many myths about academic advisement. The most common of these myths is that advisement and scheduling are one and the same. Nothing could be further from the truth. However, advisors who think this way will probably see you briefly, check the courses you have chosen for the coming semester, and either approve or disapprove them, based on the academic regulations in force for your major. If you ask for advice on a specific course, the answer may be, "Take it if you want. It will count on your record." But such advisors almost never take the time to discuss options on course selection with you. They don't feel that's their job.

Another myth about advisement has to do with the fact that your professors went to college at a time when things were different.

Academic programs offered fewer options; you signed up for the courses listed in the catalog, and that was that. Furthermore, a smaller percentage of the population attended college 20 years ago, and more of them came from families that already included at least one college graduate. For these reasons, many faculty cannot imagine why college students—even freshman students—need to sit down and talk about their concerns.

To make matters more complex, most faculty members lead busy professional lives. Remember our discussion earlier of how faculty members spend their time? For some strange reason, even though they may each have 50 to 60 students assigned for advisement, they find they have little time left in the day to complete advisement tasks properly. Consequently, students visiting advisors may feel unduly rushed through the procedure and may therefore hesitate to raise important issues which could take substantial amounts of time.

■ REALITIES OF ADVISING IN THE 1980s

"We as teachers have a greater responsibility for providing meaningful academic advising then ever before," claims David R. Hiley, Chairperson, Department of Philosophy, Memphis State University. Explaining the significance of the academic advisor to the college student of today, Hiley claims that one duty of an academic advisor is to help a student balance courses in the liberal arts with what he calls "job-specific education." Hiley says of the academic advisor: "We have the earliest contact and the best opportunity, and we can exercise more influence on students than anyone else on campus."

Unfortunately, the quality of advising is not always what it should be because many faculty tend to think of advising as scheduling and treat it as an administrative chore concerned with class schedules and requirements. It is the rare faculty member who provides really meaningful career advice to students. We want you to think of advisement as a relationship in which you do your part to make it work so that both parties benefit.

Advisement is a developmental process, not an event. It should certainly go beyond course selection, should encompass career development and the student's involvement on campus, at least with respect to major-related activities. Furthermore, the most critical time for advisement is probably at the time the student—the freshman or transfer—enters a major. Colleges erroneously assume that this student has made a reasoned decision and is totally committed to that major. In truth, most students, by and large, face great indecision in this respect, and justifiably so. Most people your age are unable to decide what they want to do for the rest of their lives, and may need to try several academic approaches before they discover one that suits them. See Step 11 for additional reasons not to rush into an academic major.

Advisement, when you think about it, is the only service colleges offer to the student that allows a continuing one-on-one relationship with a faculty member. And just look at the diverse populations entering our colleges and universities in the eighties! Collectively, they represent a much broader slice of the population at large than colleges have ever had to contend with. Then there are the variety of choices: majors, cognates, electives. It's no wonder most students need assistance in selecting courses for the coming semester. Even advisors need to check carefully to be certain they are following the latest changes in academic requirements!

■ THE REAL VALUE OF GOOD ADVISEMENT

If you are fortunate enough to have an advisor who makes you feel comfortable about talking to him, who listens to your needs before jumping in with a pat answer, and who knows whom to contact when he can't help you, you're a very lucky person. The real value of good advisement goes far beyond having an individual who will help you choose courses for the coming semester. We regard advisement as another form of teaching, and one that has advantages over classroom teaching because it is done on a one-on-one basis. Granted, seeing students in this manner puts a tremendous burden on the advisor, especially if he is responsible for a large number of students. But advisors who care and who understand the value of this process seem to make the time.

A good advisor is one who will help you understand the importance of a college education, who will "talk straight" to you about your options in your chosen academic field, who will help you assess your strengths and weaknesses in that field, and who, sometimes, will just be a good listener when you need to get something off your chest. Your advisor may not know all the answers—if he claims he does, be cautious!—but he will certainly know whom to contact for help. That contact may be an administrator in the college, a psychologist in the counseling center, a career planning specialist in the career center, or even an academic advisor in another department.

■ CHARACTERISTICS OF A GOOD ADVISOR

Although you can't tell your advisor how to behave, you can recognize the following positive traits and seek advisors who exhibit them. Remember, if you can't get along with your advisor, or don't think he's doing his job, you have a right to go to the head of your department and ask for a different advisor.

A competent advisor, first and foremost, makes time to see you and listens attentively to what you have to say. Although he may have a busy schedule, he manages to make time for you, and never attempts to rush you through an appointment. When he promises to be there, you can be certain he *will* be there.

Another quality of a good advisor is the ability to make you feel comfortable in his office. To show you that you have his complete attention, he shuts his office door so that there will be no interruptions. He may even cancel his phone calls, or answer any calls by excusing himself temporarily and taking care of the caller as quickly as possible.

He will always see you alone, not with one or two of his colleagues sitting around in his office. He will probably prefer that your friends not "hang around" while the two of you are talking either. A good advisor also recognizes that he can help you feel more comfortable by arranging his office so that there are no physical barriers (such as his desk) between you and him. When you think about the offices you have visited that seemed the most inviting, you will probably recall that they were the ones where the desk was against the wall, and the occupant of the office could sit face-to-face with you instead of behind that large block of wood or steel!

A good advisor may even use soft lighting to make his office more comfortable—for himself and for you. His walls may be filled with clues to his "other life" as a swimmer, golfer, lover of films and music, and winner of teaching awards. It's an indication that he realizes that communication is easier and more natural when the setting is right.

A good advisor always makes eye contact when he is listening or talking to you. He doesn't work at his computer terminal, grade quizzes, or gather his notes for his next lecture as long as you have the floor. He indicates his respect for you by giving you his full attention. He practices the art of "active listening," which means that whenever he isn't sure he has heard you correctly, he will play your remarks back to you to be certain you're both on the same wavelength.

Before offering you advice, a good advisor will ask you what ideas you might have. Many times, you will discover that advice isn't really what you're seeking from this person, but that you need someone you respect to validate your ideas, or concur with them. Your advisor realizes this and will attempt not to influence you unduly if he feels you have command of the situation. He will attempt to assess your ideas honestly and to respond in a manner that will help you work things through. Through this process, he may be trying to help you realize that you are able to make decisions on your own, but that it pays to have a sounding board for your ideas before you act on them. This is a very adult way to handle decision making, by the way.

A good advisor never guesses at answers. He says, "I don't know the answer to that one, but I'll see if I can find out." Depending on how long he has been teaching at your college or university, he may know exactly whom to call for the answer you need. If you have a personal problem, he may refer you to a psychologist at the counseling center. If you question your choice of majors, he may direct you to a career counselor or to an advisor in a department that may be of interest to you. If you are in the position of visiting an advisor in another department to determine if his program of study will meet your needs, he will resist any "recruitment" techniques until he has determined from your remarks whether or not his field of study is what you are actually talking about.

Finally, a good advisor protects his own privacy while making himself accessible to his advisees. He may ask that you not call him at home, unless there is an emergency. He may insist that you call in advance to schedule an appointment, so that he can tend to his other obligations without interruption. He may not always be in his office, but you should be aware of his hours from the note he posts outside his door.

■ PREPARING FOR AN ADVISEMENT APPOINTMENT

You will be even more comfortable talking with your advisor if you take a few moments to prepare yourself for the meeting. If the purpose of your meeting is to have your classes approved for the coming semester, have the necessary paperwork completed before you show up. This might include a list of courses you are currently taking and a list of proposed courses for the coming semester. You might also list alternate courses to ask about. If your college asks that you pick up your student folder and bring it to your advisement meeting, you should allow extra time to do this, since "front offices" tend to be busy places and you may have to wait a few moments before you can sign out your records. You certainly want to show up on time, and once you're in the office, you want to get down to business. If the advisor wants to chat, let him initiate the conversation. If not, get down to business. By the same token, if you need to be somewhere else soon, let him know that if the pace of the meeting seems to have slowed down.

If your meeting has to do with problems in a specific course, or other events in your life that are affecting your academic performance negatively, review the situation in your mind before you walk in, and simply share your concerns about your classes with your advisor. You will know in the first few minutes whether the person you are facing is going to be empathetic by the way he looks at you and listens to you. A good advisor will give you a chance to get the whole story out before interrupting, and will then try to determine what the next logical step might be. If he is skilled in interpersonal relationships, he will communicate in an understanding manner and either help you find the answers you seek, or send you to a different sort of professional for help.

■ ADVISEMENT AS TEACHING

What advisement boils down to is this: simply another form of teaching; for this reason alone it needs to be carried out in a first-rate manner. An advisor can help a student avoid many of the pitfalls and anxieties that all too often can have a negative impact on achievements in the classroom. Furthermore, your advisor can serve as one of those special people each of us needs throughout life. During your college years, he's certainly equipped to fill that role. As mentor, friend, and counselor, he can provide you with an understanding and patient ear, wise advice, and self-esteem—and those aren't bad things to have when you're working for your degree!

As much learning—and often more—can take place in the advisor's office as in the classroom. That's something you—and your advisor—need to remember.

■ EXERCISE 1

RATING YOUR ADVISOR

The next time you visit your advisor, take mental notes about the meeting. After you leave his or her office, fill out the following checklist and share it with other students, as you compare with them their own experiences with their advisors.

RATING MY ADVISEMENT CONFERENCE

_____ 1. The advisor listened to me thoroughly before attempting to provide answers.

_____ 2. I felt comfortable before we began our discussion.

_____ 3. The door to the office was closed to assure privacy.

_____ 4. There were few—or no—interruptions.

_____ 5. The advisor did not sit behind a desk.

_____ 6. The advisor looked at me during the meeting.

_____ 7. The advisor paraphrased some of my words to make certain he (or she) had heard me correctly.

_____ 8. The advisor asked for my ideas before attempting to solve my problems for me.

_____ 9. The advisor treated me with respect.

_____ 10. I did not feel rushed during the meeting.

_____ 11. The advisor called on other resources when he (or she) did not feel qualified to answer my question.

■ EXERCISE 2

GIVING THANKS WHERE
THANKS ARE DUE

If you have been fortunate enough to have found a good advisor, you should let him or her know. Shortly after your appointment, write a personal note to your advisor, telling how he or she helped you. Be specific; a simple "thank you for seeing me," while polite, will not be appreciated nearly as much as a remark such as, "You really helped me make a decision about whether or not to study a foreign language, " or "Just letting me talk about my problems has helped me see how to overcome them." Get in the habit of thanking people in writing for favors. You will find them even more receptive the next time you make a visit.

■ EXERCISE 3

SHAPING THE IDEAL ADVISOR RELATIONSHIP

In small-group discussions, share your thoughts about what con-
stitutes ideal advisement with others. Have a member of the group
record the thoughts of all group members on this subject, and then
have each group in the class share its list with other groups. You
should make one list of characteristics of a good advisor, and a
second list of characteristics of a good advisee.

STEP 11

YOUR PRESENT ACADEMIC MAJOR, YOUR FUTURE CAREER

We have talked about the many myths that exist about college, but perhaps the one that can be the most harmful, by far, is the myth of the academic major as a guarantee of a specific future career. College can prepare you for many careers, and it is this fact that makes college different from the kind of education you would receive at a technical school. There, you might study welding and become a welder. At a four-year college, the goal is to prepare you for any number of things, depending on your own aptitude and ambitions.

Part of the "major myth" leads many young people (and their parents) to believe that you have to study business to have a career in business or journalism to have a career in newspaper work, and that degrees in such esoteric subjects as English, history, or philosophy are of no practical value whatsoever. Nothing could be further from the truth. Many a bank president majored in English, history, or music, and you will find many other successful career people who chose a college major that seemed to have little or nothing to do with their ultimate careers. One of your authors, for example, majored in journalism, learned the elements of reporting, and decided when he graduated that working for a newspaper or magazine was the last thing on earth he wanted to do. But, using his skills as a writer, he landed a job in advertising, and that became his chosen career until he entered teaching during a mid-life career change. Your other author majored in history and is presently an associate vice-president at his university. Both authors happen to have the same master's degree in a field called American civilization. Could you have predicted their present careers from their college majors?

■ THE PRESSURE TO MAJOR

With the best of intentions, parents, friends, and other relatives tell us how important it is to choose the right major prior to beginning college. We know of a young man in the tenth grade who was told by his history teacher that he needed to choose a college major as soon as possible, since he would begin college in less than two years! Certainly, it's easier to enter college with that decision made, but what if it isn't the right decision? Your authors weren't certain what they wanted to be when they started college. Are you?

■ THE BEAUTY OF A LIBERAL EDUCATION

We spoke earlier of the advantages of a liberal eduation. Now let's relate that to your career concerns. A recent survey was done among successful business leaders, who were asked what qualities they looked for most in job applicants. Their answer surprised many young people, for what was most important to these successful leaders was not knowledge in a specific career field, but such things as the ability to reason, the ability to express oneself clearly and forcefully in writing, the ability to carry on an intelligent conversation with others, and a broad-based knowledge of the world they live in. In other words, they were seeking those basic human skills that are learned from reading great works of literature; developing an appreciation for theatre, art, and music; and learning to reason through an awareness of some of the great philosophers in history. The practical skills became secondary to these universal traits of an educated person.

■ HOW, THEN, TO CHOOSE A MAJOR?

Obviously, despite what we have just said, many college students do choose academic majors in specific career fields, such as business, journalism, pharmacy, nursing, computer science, and engineering, and most of them do quite well. Many others, however, choose a field such as history, chemistry, government, Spanish, English, philosophy, psychology, or speech, simply because they like one of these areas and have always done well in it. Not surprisingly, these are two of the considerations for choosing a major. First, you should enjoy what you are studying. Secondly, you should have some aptitude in that field. Even though everyone tells you that engineers are making more money than anyone else, it makes no sense for you to choose engineering if (a) you don't enjoy it and (b) you can't understand a thing in class. It reminds us of a student who wanted to major in advertising because he heard it was a glamorous profession, but firmly stated that he hated to write and wanted to do "something else" in advertising. After we explained that writing was a key skill in any field of mass communications, he sought another major.

Career planners speak of interests, skills, aptitudes, personality, and life goals/work values as the determinants of success in your academic major and career. Because no two individuals are alike in any of these respects, it may be dangerous to take the advice of a well-meaning friend or family member when it's time to declare a major.

■ INTERESTS

Interests develop from previous experiences and from assumptions you make about things. You may want to write for the college newspaper because you did it in high school and loved it, or you'd like to try it because other people seem to enjoy doing it. Your interests may change as you grow and change. To get a clearer picture of your interests, you can take a number of standardized personality inventories at your counseling center. You can also:

1. Read your college catalog and check each course that sounds interesting to you. Ask yourself why they sound interesting.

2. Make a list of classes, activities, clubs, etc., you enjoyed in high school. Ask yourself why you enjoyed them.

■ SKILLS

Skills are things you do well. You can't claim to be a good writer unless you've written something good. Like interests, skills can be developed. You may choose to use the resources at your college to improve your writing. Other skills you have may include reading, conversing, socializing, teaching, entertaining, planning, repairing things, solving problems, listening, observing, being tactful, or directing others.

■ APTITUDES

Aptitudes are inherent strengths which may be inherited, or may have emerged from your early learning environment. Having an aptitude for something doesn't ensure success, any more than having a skill or interest might. But coupled with high motivation and hard work, aptitude breeds success. At the same time, high motivation and hard work alone may not be able to compensate for low aptitude. You may study calculus for hours and still barely make a C.

It makes sense to build on those aptitudes you are strongest in. A sample of aptitudes might include reasoning ability, mechanical ability, clerical speed, clerical accuracy, language usage, or numerical ability.

■ PERSONALITY CHARACTERISTICS

The personality characteristics that make you a unique individual can't be ignored in the career decision process. If you are quiet, orderly, neat, calm, and detailed, you will probably make a different work choice than the person who is aggressive, outgoing, argumentative, and witty. Are you academic, daring, cooperative, intellectual, logical, energetic, calm, forceful, modest, good-natured, emotional, meticulous, curious, or what? Making an assessment of your personality may give you important clues to the kinds of work you love and hate.

■ LIFE GOALS/WORK VALUES

Though most of us want success and satisfaction in life, each of us defines these things differently. Success and satisfaction are directly related to the knowledge that we are achieving the life goals we have set for ourselves and valuing what we receive from our work. Someone, for example, whose life goal is to help society may make a far different career choice than someone whose life goal is to compete with others or to pursue knowledge for its own sake. By the same token, someone whose work values include change and variety may not be happy in a job which restricts one to a daily routine, while someone seeking independence in a career may not be able to perform under constant supervision.

■ CAREER CHOICES

The federal government lists more than 31,000 career fields. While you certainly can't explore all of them, you can focus your search on the most appropriate careers for you. Dr. John Holland, a psychologist at Johns Hopkins University, has developed a system based on several factors designed to help you identify career possibilities. His system divides people into six general categories, based on differences in their interests, skills, values, and personality characteristics. His categories are:

1. *Realistic.* Realistic people are competitive and assertive, and show interest in things that require motor coordination, skill, and physical strength. They like to take a concrete approach to problem solving rather than rely on abstract theory, and tend to be interested in scientific or mechanical, rather than cultural and aesthetic, areas.

2. *Investigative.* Investigative people prefer to think rather than to act; to organize and understand rather than to persuade. They are not apt to be people-oriented.

3. *Artistic.* Artistic people value self-expression, dislike structure, prefer tasks involving personal or physical skills, and are more likely to express emotion than other types.

4. *Social.* Social people seem to satisfy their needs in a teaching or helping situation. In contrast to investigative and realistic people, the social type is drawn more to close interpersonal relationships and is less apt to engage in intellectual or extensive physical activity.

5. *Enterprising.* Enterprising people use their well-developed verbal skills to persuade, rather than support, others. They also values prestige and status, and are more likely to pursue them than are conventional people.

6. *Conventional.* Conventional people don't mind working under rules and regulations, and emphasize their self-control. They prefer structure and order to ambiguity in work and interpersonal situations, and place high value on prestige or status.

Not surprisingly, Holland has organized career fields into these same six categories, each representing a specific set of skills, personality characteristics, interests, and values. As you read the following examples, see how your career interests match the category as described above.

- *Realistic:* agricultural engineer, barber, dairy farmer, electrical contractor, ferryboat captain, gem cutter, heavy equipment operator, industrial arts teacher, jeweler, navy officer, health and safety specialist, radio repairer, sheet metal worker, tailor, waitress/waiter.

- *Investigative:* urban planner, chemical engineer, bacteriologist, cattle-breeding technician, ecologist, flight engineer, genealogist, handwriting analyst, laboratory science worker, marine scientist, nuclear medical technologist, obstetrician, quality control technician, sanitation scientist, TV repairer, balloon pilot.

- *Artistic:* architect, film editor/director, actor, cartoonist, interior decorator, fashion model, furrier, graphic communications specialist, jewelry designer, journalist, medical illustrator, editor, orchestra leader, public relations specialist, sculptor.

- *Social:* nurse, teacher, caterer, dental assistant, social worker, genetic counselor, hair stylist, home economist, job analyst, marriage counselor, parole officer, rehabilitation counselor, school superintendent, theatre manager, production expediter.

- *Enterprising:* banker, city manager, employment interviewer, FBI agent, health administrator, industrial relations director, judge, labor arbitrator, personnel assistant, TV announcer, salary and wage administrator, insurance salesperson, sales engineer, telephone interviewer, travel guide.

- *Conventional:* accountant, statistician, census enumerator, data processor, dental assistant, hospital admitting officer, instrument assembler, insurance records supervisor, keypunch operator, legal secretary, library assistant, linotype operator, mail clerk, office coordinator, reservation agent.

While Holland's model may seem to be a simple method for matching people to careers, it was never meant for that purpose. Rather, it was intended to help you answer some questions about career choices in two ways. First, you can begin to identify many career fields that are consistent with what you know about yourself. Once you've identified potential fields, you can use the career library at your college to get as much information as possible about those fields. Information you should seek would include daily activities for specific jobs, interests and abilities required, preparation needed for an entry-level job, working conditions, salary and benefits, and employment outlook.

Second, you can begin to identify the harmony or conflicts in your career choices, based on what you know about your interests, aptitudes, personality characteristics, and life goals/work values.

Perhaps the best advice about your future career that we can offer you as you begin your college years is this: Rather than approach college as a "career factory," think of it in a much broader sense.

Realize that there is no shame in not knowing how you want to spend the rest of your life when you're 18 years old. Some individuals have problems making this decision when they're 50! If you are uncertain about choosing an academic major, it may be best for you to begin in a liberal arts program, and to seek career counseling at your college. It isn't unusual to change majors in your second year of college. Somehow, after you have sampled from the tree of knowledge for a few semesters, the choice of a major tends to make more sense and become much easier.

EXERCISE 1
FIELD RESEARCH ON CAREERS AND MAJORS

Choose several career fields (not fewer than three) that are of some interest to you and interview a professional in each of these. This may consist of calling a person in your town or city and setting up an appointment, or writing someone in another city if you cannot locate someone in a particular field in your town. During the interview, be certain to find out what this person's academic major was in college, and how he or she has applied that course of study to present and former jobs. Perhaps someone you choose did not attend college; that's all right, too. In that case, find out how he or she learned the needed skills for the job. During your chat, you might also try to find out something about that person's interests, skills, aptitudes, personality characteristics, and life goals/work values. In your report, tell what you have learned from this exercise.

EXERCISE 2
PERSONALITY MOSAIC[1]

Circle the numbers of the statements that clearly feel like something you might say or do or think—something that feels like you.

---

1. Betty Neville Michelozzi. *Coming Alive from Nine to Five*, Second Edition. Palo Alto, Calif.: Mayfield Publishing Co., © 1980, 1984. Used by permission of the publisher.

When you have finished, circle the same number on the answer grid on p. 109.

1. It's important for me to have a strong, agile body.

2. I need to understand things thoroughly.

3. Music, color, beauty of any kind can really affect my moods.

4. People enrich my life and give it meaning.

5. I have confidence in myself that I can make things happen.

6. I appreciate clear directions so I know exactly what I can do.

7. I can usually carry/build/fix things myself.

8. I can get absorbed for hours in thinking something out.

9. I appreciate beautiful surroundings; color and design mean a lot to me.

10. I love company.

11. I enjoy competing.

12. I need to get my surroundings in order before I start a project.

13. I enjoy making things with my hands.

14. It's satisfying to explore new ideas.

15. I always seem to be looking for new ways to express my creativity.

16. I value being able to share personal concerns with people.

17. Being a key person in a group is very satisfying to me.

18. I take pride in being very careful about all the details of my work.

19. I don't mind getting my hands dirty.

20. I see education as a lifelong process of developing and sharpening my mind.

21. I love to dress in unusual ways, to try new colors and styles.

22. I can often sense when a person needs to talk to someone.

23. I enjoy getting people organized and on the move.

24. A good routine helps me get the job done.

25. I like to buy sensible things that I can make or work on myself.

26. Sometimes I can sit for hours and work on puzzles or read or just think about life.

27. I have a great imagination.

28. It makes me feel good to take care of people.

29. I like to have people rely on me to get the job done.

30. I'm satisfied knowing that I've done an assignment carefully and completely.

31. I'd rather be on my own doing practical, hands-on activities.

32. I'm eager to read about any subject that arouses my curiosity.

33. I love to try creative new ideas.

34. If I have a problem with someone, I prefer to talk it out and resolve it.

35. To be successful, it's important to aim high.

36. I prefer being in a position where I don't have to take responsibility for decisions.

37. I don't enjoy spending a lot of time discussing things. What's right is right.

38. I need to analyze a problem pretty thoroughly before I act on it.

39. I like to rearrange my surroundings to make them unique and different.

40. When I feel down, I find a friend to talk to.

41. After I suggest a plan, I prefer to let others take care of the details.

42. I'm usually content where I am.

43. It's invigorating to do things outdoors.

44. I keep asking "why."

45. I like my work to be an expression of my moods and feelings.

46. I like to find ways to help people care more for each other.

47. It's exciting to take part in important decisions.

48. I'm always glad to have someone else take charge.

49. I like my surroundings to be plain and practical.

50. I need to stay with a problem until I figure out an answer.

51. The beauty of nature touches something deep inside me.

52. Close relationships are important to me.

53. Promotion and advancement are important to me.

54. Efficiency, for me, means doing a set amount carefully each day.

55. A strong system of law and order is important to preserve chaos.

56. Thought-provoking books always broaden my perspective.

57. I look forward to seeing art shows, plays, and good films.

58. I haven't seen you for so long. I'd love to know what you're doing.

59. It's exciting to be able to influence people.

60. Good, hard physical work never hurt anyone.

61. When I say I'll do it, I follow through on every detail.

62. I'd like to learn all there is to know about subjects that interest me.

63. I don't want to be like everyone else. I like to do things differently.

64. Tell me how I can help you.

65. I'm willing to take some risks to get ahead.

66. I like exact directions and clear rules when I start something new.

67. The first thing I look for in a car is a well-built engine.

68. Those people are intellectually stimulating.

69. When I'm creating, I tend to let everything else go.

70. I feel concerned that so many people in our society need help.

71. It's fun to get ideas across to people.

72. I hate it when they keep changing the system just when I get it down.

73. I usually know how to take care of things in an emergency.

74. Just reading about new discoveries is exciting.

75. I like to create happenings.

76. I often go out of my way to pay attention to people who seem lonely and friendless.

77. I love to bargain.

78. I don't like to do things unless I'm sure they're approved.

79. Sports are important in building strong bodies.

80. I've always been curious about the way nature works.

81. It's fun to be in a mood to try to do something unusual.

82. I believe that people are basically good.

83. If I don't make it the first time, I usually bounce back with energy and enthusiasm.

84. I appreciate knowing exactly what people expect of me.

85. I like to take things apart to see if I can fix them.

86. Don't get excited. We can think it out and plan the right move logically.

87. It would be hard to imagine my life without beauty around me.

88. People often seem to tell me their problems.

89. I can usually connect with people who get me in touch with a network of resources.

90. I don't need much to be happy.

Now circle the same numbers below that you circled above.

R	I	A	S	E	C
1	2	3	4	5	6
7	8	9	10	11	12
13	14	15	16	17	18
19	20	21	22	23	24
25	26	27	28	29	30
31	32	33	34	35	36
37	38	39	40	41	42
43	44	45	46	47	48
49	50	51	52	53	54
55	56	57	58	59	60
61	62	63	64	65	66
67	68	69	70	71	72
73	74	75	76	77	78
79	80	81	82	83	84
85	86	87	88	89	90

Now add up the number of circles in each column.

R ____ I ____ A ____ S ____ E ____ C ____

Which are your three highest scores?

1st ____ 2nd ____ 3rd ____

Now go back and re-read the descriptions of these three types and see how accurately they describe you!

STEP 12

USING YOUR COLLEGE LIBRARY FOR BETTER PAPERS, ENHANCED LEARNING, AND HIGHER GRADES

For those of you who come to college from small towns, a college library can be an awesome experience. Floor after floor of books, some in languages you don't recognize, seem to create an unending maze in which you wander aimlessly, seeking a simple reference on tobacco farming in the late nineteenth century, and finding that many of the sources you were seeking have been checked out by others.

If your library has a well-stocked reference section on the main floor, you may wonder why so much room has been devoted to books you can't even check out, why an entire shelf is filled with telephone directories from around the U.S., or why so many students are spending so much time copying things out of books that seem no more than guides to other books.

Yes, libraries can be frustrating when you don't know where to go first, and that's the point of this section of your step-by-step guide. There is a right way and many wrong ways to get the most out of your library. It isn't more difficult to conduct a literature search the right way; in fact, it's easier when you realize how profitable it will be. It's simply that most of us were never taught how to use a library properly. We aim to correct this in the next few pages.

In fact, most of this section consists of an exercise in which you are directed through a library search. The topic you choose doesn't matter. It's the method you use to gather the information that does.

Before we begin, we want to stress the value of knowing how to use your library properly.

■ THE VALUE OF THE PAST

It has been said that by studying the past, we learn not to make the same mistakes that were made by our ancestors. We also develop a greater understanding of how present-day ideas, philosophies, and institutions came to be, and, through that understanding, are better able to cope with them or cause them to change. Where does the past reside? In the writing of others, some of whom lived centuries ago and others who are of our generation but have chronicled the events of the past through meticulous research. Your professors and textbooks can only begin to scratch the surface of this rich heritage that touches each of us, and for many subjects, perhaps this is enough. But if you have a special interest in a certain field, you will want to find out as much about it as you can. You may even discover new ways of putting old information together that shed a new light on a long-forgotten event. This is the inherent drama of discovery, of finding new knowledge from that which already exists, and the library is where your search begins.

■ THE INFORMATION EXPLOSION

This need to search for the answers to today's questions by exploring the past has become even more complex today because of the tremendous increase in information over the last several years. The influence of the computer has caused information and knowledge to grow at an astonishing speed, resulting in an explosion of records in paper, microfiche, and electronic formats. This makes it tougher and tougher to keep up, even in a very narrow area of knowledge, and it makes the search for information in a large library all the more frustrating if you don't know where to begin. The purpose of the following exercise is to show you not only where to begin, but to guide you through each step in

a logical fashion, so that you will know how to conduct research on any topic merely by following this guide. Sound simple? It is.

But first, we need to define a number of sources of information in
your library, so that you will be prepared to use them properly.

■ ENCYCLOPEDIAS

If you are beginning a search on an unfamiliar topic, general or
special encyclopedias can give you the foundation you need to
understand some complex issues. These volumes are designed to
lead you to other sources, as you will soon discover. You should
also know that there is a special subject encyclopedia covering
almost every discipline.

■ DICTIONARIES

If you need a word defined in a very special context, there is
probably a special subject dictionary available to you.

■ BOOKS

As you build upon information from encyclopedias, you will move
to more detailed sources, such as books. The key to a library's book
collection is its catalog, sometimes available in card form or com-
puterized form.

■ BIBLIOGRAPHIES

These lists supply you with more sources to consult. Normally, you
look in a bibliography to see if any sources on your topic exist, and
then you check the library's catalog or magazine holdings to see if
the cited sources are available.

■ INDEXES AND ABSTRACTS

These put you in touch with magazine and book articles on your topic. Periodical indexes offer you access to recent information. Abstracts refer you to currently produced information and also include a summary or critique of the source referred to. There are indexes and abstracts covering every field of inquiry. One helpful feature of indexes is that they will let you find the opinions or thoughts that existed at a specific time. Just check the indexes for the appropriate years.

■ LIBRARIANS

Approaching a librarian is an important step in seeking information. Librarians may look busy all the time, even grouchy once in a while, but they really do enjoy helping people. Otherwise, they wouldn't be in the business. Librarians are paid to provide service to you, first and foremost. So, walk right up to a librarian, smile, and ask your questions.

During your college years, you will be asked to research a number of topics for various class assignments. You can do a superficial job and earn an average grade—or you can discover how to do a thorough job, and probably earn a much higher one. Few freshmen realize how much information a library contains, or how to read the "road maps" leading to such information. This exercise, developed by our friend, Professor Charles Curran of the USC College of Library and Information Science, points the way to getting the most information available for the topic of your choice.

◼ EXERCISE 1

THE LIBRARY SEARCH, FROM A TO Z

First, you'll need a topic. Choose one of your own, or from this list:

Schizophrenia
Paranoia
Sea monsters
Penology
Autism
Republican Party
Love
Prejudice
Hypnosis
The Reformation
Capital punishment
The Great Depression
The Women's Movement
Cybernetics
Crime prevention
Nuclear power
Protectionism and foreign trade
The politicization of the Olympics
Agribusiness
Unions

Democratic Party
Moving pictures—history
Radio astronomy
Mafia
Air pollution
Stock market
Slang
Occult
Therapeutic abortion
The Moral Majority
Pornography
Venereal disease
KKK
Africa
Militarism
Legalized prostitution
Christian values
Employment (jobs for us?)
Witchcraft
Information explosion

This exercise will take you through the following source materials.
You will probably find all of these in the reference section of your
library.

1. General encyclopedias

2. Subject encyclopedias

3. *Library of Congress List of Subject Headings*

4. *Readers' Guide to Periodicals*

5. Subject indexes

6. Abstracts

7. *Editorials on File*

8. *The New York Times* Index

The reference section should be staffed by one or more reference librarians who are there to help you with your search. If you get stuck, ask for their help. It's their job to provide such assistance. The reference section contains guides to other references, as you will soon find out. Books in the reference section may not be checked out because they are in great demand and require a minimal amount of reading time compared to the reference works they will lead you to.

The eight source materials above begin with general references and proceed step-by-step to specific references. As you progress from general encyclopedias to subject encyclopedias, for example, see how much more data become available about your topic. If in doubt as to where to find some of these sources, ask the reference librarian. Once you learn where the sources are, you can come back to them easily. Now it's time to begin.

1. Select any general encyclopedia (*Americana, Brittanica, Colliers, World Book,* etc.) and look in the index volume for your topic. Report what you find in terms of references to that topic.

   Topic _____

   Encyclopedia _____ Index page _____

   In what volumes and on what pages will you find information on this topic?

VOL	PAGE	REFERENCE TERM (WATCH FOR CROSS REFERENCES)
___	___	_____
___	___	_____
___	___	_____
___	___	_____

Would this information help you discuss the topic in class or write a paper on the topic? Explain why or why not.

2. Select any appropriate subject encyclopedia (*Encyclopedia of Philosophy, International Encyclopedia of the Social Sciences, Encyclopedia of Religion and Ethics, McGraw-Hill Encyclopedia of Science and Technology* are examples) and search again for your topic.

Topic _____

Encyclopedia _____ Index page_____

In what volumes and on what pages will you find information on this topic?

Vol.	Page	Reference Term (Watch For Cross References)
____	____	_____
____	____	_____
____	____	_____
____	____	_____

Would this information help you discuss the topic in class or write a paper on the topic? Explain why or why not.

3. Look in the *Library of Congress List of Subject Headings (LC)* for your topic. Remember to continue to search for the same topic throughout this exercise.

Topic _____

Does the *LC* indicate that this topic is an official index term?

Yes ____ No ____

If no, official term as listed here is _____

What cross-references does *LC* suggest you also check?

_____

_____

Locate and inspect two books on the subject supplied by the *LC*.

Term from *LC* list _____

Book call number _____ Book title _____

Why would this book help me or not help me with my paper?

Term from *LC* _____

Book call number _____ Book title _____

Why would this book help me or not help me with my paper?

4. Check the *Readers' Guide* (*RG*) for magazine or journal articles on your topic.

   Date of *RG* _____ Term searched _____

   If this term is not an official index term in *RG*, list the ones which *RG* recommends you use: _____

   _____

   Article I

   Article title _____

   Name of journal or magazine _____

   Volume ____ Date _____ Pages _____

   Article II

   Article title _____

   Name of journal or magazine _____

   Volume ____ Date _____ Pages_____

   Check the serials list to see if your library subscribes to these periodicals and, if so, record the call numbers:

   _____

   Find the magazines or journals. Would these articles help you write about or discuss your topic? Why or why not?

5. Now check a subject index such as *Social Science Index, Business Periodicals Index, Nursing Index, Education Index, Public Affairs Information Service, Music Index,* or *Humanities Index.* Ask which indexes are appropriate for your topic. Find an article listed in the index.

Name of subject index used _____

Title of article found in index _____

Name and date of periodical in which article appears _____

Does your library subscribe? ____ If so, get call number _____

If the article is available, find it and explain its value to you. Will it help you or not? Why?

6. Find any abstract which appears to relate to your topic. Again, seek help to be certain you have checked all pertinent abstracts in your library. Examples of abstracts: *International Political Science Abstracts, Resources in Education, Psychological Abstracts, Sociological Abstracts, America: History and Life, and Political Science Abstracts.*

Name of abstract used _____

Term under which you found article on your topic _____

Title of article found in abstract _____

Read the abstract. Does it sound as though it would be helpful to you? Why? What does it say that indicates a possible use for the article?

If the abstract sounds as if the article would be of help, complete the next section.

Name and date of periodical in which article appears _____

Does your library subscribe? ____ If so, get call number _____

If the article is available, find it and explain its value to you. Will it help you or not? Why?

_____

_____

7. Check *Editorials on File.* Start with the most recent issues and use the indexes. Work back in time from the most recent index. Check at least five years of *Editorials on File.* This unique publication will provide you with a variety of viewpoints from the nation's leading newspapers about your topic.

   Is your topic ever listed? ____ . If so, report generally on the amount of information available to you. Would this material help your research? Why?

8. Check *The New York Times Index.* Start with the most recent index and work back five years. Is there any coverage for your topic? If so, copy a citation and take it to the micro area or wherever newspapers are filed in your library. Ask for help in locating the microfilm and loading it in the reader. Would this article help your research? Why?

   When you have completed this exercise, tell in your own words how it has helped you gain a greater understanding of your library and the research methods that will help you prepare better papers.

STEP 13

FINDING THE MONEY FOR COLLEGE. MANAGING IT AFTER YOU GET THERE.

The cost of attending college has been rising faster than the cost of living, and today's inflated living costs certainly have taken a chunk out of the budgets of most Americans. Small wonder that most families need to make plans well in advance of their son's or daughter's college years to determine how to pay for tuition, books, and the many other expenses involved in getting a college education.

If you have entered, or are about to enter college, your family probably has already begun to make plans for financing your education. Therefore, we want to concentrate on the costs of attending college rather than on the procedures for applying for financial assistance. Then we'll attempt to provide you with a helpful plan for managing your expenses once you begin college.

■ COSTS OF COLLEGE

Tuition and other academic fees are the most obvious costs of attending college, and are fairly easy to determine, but you will discover that many other expenses are involved, and some are more difficult to assess. In addition to tuition, you should plan to spend money on books, equipment, or supplies, room and board, transportation, plus personal or miscellaneous items.

You will find your college catalog helpful when you attempt to determine these costs. Your admissions and financial aid offices can also assist you in this respect. The financial aid office should be able to supply you with the average comprehensive costs most students face for the current academic year. Using this as a start, you can begin to plan your own budget, accepting fixed costs such as tuition, and attempting to reduce other costs. For example, purchasing used books instead of new ones can save you money. If you must commute, is carpooling or public transportation an option to owning your own car? Will you be paying for courses by the credit hour, or can you pay a fixed tuition fee as a full-time student that allows you to take more hours without additional cost? Can you save money by earning advanced placement in courses through examination, thus eliminating your need to register for and complete such courses? Is a board plan available that is less costly than paying on a per-meal basis?

Once you know what the academic year is actually going to cost you, the next step is to determine whether your financial resources are enough to meet those expenses.

▪ PERSONAL/FAMILY RESOURCES

First, you should identify personal and family resources available to help pay for your education. Savings, insurance policies taken out for you when you were younger, trust funds, and summer employment may contribute to your college fund. Savings from part-time jobs may also help. After identifying the personal/family funds available to you, you may discover a gap between what you have and what you need. At this point, it's time to think about applying for financial aid.

▪ FINANCIAL AID RESOURCES

Whether you're a freshman or an upperclass student, you will have to reapply for financial aid each year. By financial aid, we mean any type of financial support that's available to you to help pay your educational costs. Financial aid may refer to anything from a federal grant to an institutional scholarship. It may be gift aid or self-help aid. Gift aid normally means that you don't have to repay the award; self-help implies you must do something in order to receive the aid. Gift aid may be a scholarship based solely on academic merit, whereas a student loan is an example of self-help aid, since you must promise to repay the loan after finishing your education. In either case, financial need may or may not be a factor.

Typically, the criteria for financial aid are academic merit, financial need, or a combination of the two. Some academic scholarships are awarded solely on the basis of your successfully meeting certain scholastic criteria, and will be continued as long as you meet those criteria. Other scholarships require you to demonstrate financial need in order to qualify for the award.

■ TYPES OF AID AVAILABLE

Generally speaking, five basic types of financial aid are available: grants, loans, work-study programs, scholarships, and benefit programs.

Grant programs require no repayment from you, while loans require that you repay the amount you received, plus interest, when you leave school. The College Work-Study Program is a need-based financial aid program that allows you to work part-time while going to school in order to earn part of the money you'll need to pay for your educational expenses. Generally, you'll be working on the campus in a college department. Many schools also offer regular part-time student assistant jobs. In considering whether to work while attending school, you should always remember that your first priority is to succeed *academically*. If working does not adversely affect your grades, you can gain good, marketable job experience by working part-time. In fact, several studies indicate that part-time work has a positive impact on students in terms of academics and time management skills. The rule of thumb is to work no more than 20 hours a week if you are attending classes on a full-time basis (12–15 semester hours at most schools).

Many colleges and universities also offer cooperative (co-op) education programs which allow you to combine an academic program with employment in your field of study. Generally, you will be expected to work one term, attend classes the next, work the next, and so forth. This not only provides valuable work experience that can pay off when you graduate and begin job hunting, but you will also earn money, some of which you may be able to apply to the cost of your education. Co-op programs are usually administered by your campus career center.

While a number of publications can help you identify financial aid opportunities, your best source of information is the financial aid office at the college or university you have selected.

■ MANAGING YOUR MONEY

Whether you're receiving need-based financial aid or paying your own way entirely, you must learn to successfully manage your financial resources—not only in college, but for life. Managing your money in college is generally more difficult, however, because of your limited ability to earn money while you are attending classes.

The key to managing your money is planning. If you don't plan how you're going to spend your money, you risk facing some serious problems as your year progresses, and such problems may have a direct bearing on your ability to stay current in your classes. The keys to financial planning can be summed up in two words: budgeting and discipline.

■ BUDGETING MADE SIMPLE

To establish a reasonable budget for yourself, you need to determine three facts. First, how long a period of time do you want your budget to cover? Second, what items must your budget include? Third, how much money do you actually have?

The whole point of budgeting is to establish a plan for allocating the money you have available. In other words, budgeting is nothing

more than a systematic way of preventing confusion and uncertainty about how you will spend your money. Following the next
three simple steps can help you ensure a reasonable and comprehensive budget.

■ FIRST, ITEMIZE YOUR EXPENSES

To begin the process, list all the expenses you can think of. Begin
by listing such costs as tuition, fees, books, and supplies. Once you
feel you have adequately covered your educational expenses, begin
to itemize your anticipated living costs. You must include not only
such things as food, laundry, clothing, toiletries/cosmetics, etc., but
social life as well. The point is that you can be in control of your
money only if you know "up front" how much you're going to need
to spend, and for what. See Chart A.

CHART A: ITEMIZING YOUR EXPENSES

Time Period: Academic Year
A. Educational Expenses
    Tuition $500
    Fees   700
    Books   250
    Supplies   50
       Subtotal $1500
B. Living Expenses
    Housing $850
    Board   1475
    Personal   75
    Transportation   300
    Clothes   225
    Entertainment   175
       Subtotal $3100
         Total $4600

■ SECOND, ITEMIZE YOUR RESOURCES

Among the many ways to list your financial resources, we prefer
one called the category approach. Using this approach, you list the

money you will have available by categories, such as part-time work, money from parents, savings, student aid, and so on. This method provides you with a perspective of what you'll have available and where it's coming from, and also will help you when it comes time to actually write your budget. See Chart B.

CHART B: ITEMIZING YOUR RESOURCES

Time Period: Academic Year

A. Savings
Yours	$400
Parents	200

B. Parent Help
Cash	300
Bank Loans	1000

C. Work
Summer
Part-time During
  School Year

D. Benefits
Social Security
Veteran's
Other

E. Financial Aid
Grants	1200
Scholarships	400
Student Loan	600

F. Other
ROTC Pay	900
Relatives	
Trusts	
Total	$5000

■ THIRD, ORDER YOUR EXPENSES

Now go through all the costs you've listed and determine whether each can be labeled as discretionary (avoidable or nonfixed) or nondiscretionary (unavoidable or fixed). The purpose of this step is to help you focus on those costs such as tuition, books, and residence hall charges that are fixed (those you must pay for) and those such as food, clothing, and entertainment that are not fixed (those you have some control over). Once you set aside money for the nondiscretionary expenses, which are not subject to negotiation, you can focus your attention on the discretionary, or controllable, costs.

Next, rank all discretionary costs in order of their importance to you. Obviously, you can't stop eating or transporting yourself to campus, but you can decide how much you're going to spend for these items. For example, you may find that using public transportation or carpooling is one way to reduce your transportation expense. Once you have negotiated these expenses, you are finally ready to construct your budget.

■ DETERMINING YOUR BUDGET

You should actually create two versions of your budget. The first should put your financial picture in overall perspective, while the second should be an actual weekly or monthly version of how you intend to spend your money. See Chart C for an example of an overall budget for a student attending a college that operates on the typical two-semester academic year calendar. This student lives on campus and makes the short trip home for visits and holidays three times each semester.

■ BRINGING EVERYTHING INTO PERSPECTIVE

Now all that remains to be done is to keep a monthly expense budget to determine what your expenses should be for a particular month.

Keep in mind that large expenses for tuition, books, and room occur at the beginning of the semester, while continuing expenses for food, clothing, etc., occur on some sort of ongoing basis. The monthly approach is a convenient mechanism for keeping track of your money without making it overly complicated. Since checking

CHART C: EXPENSE/RESOURCE BUDGET SUMMARY

I. Itemized Expenses		II. Itemized Resources	
A. Educational		A. Savings	
Tuition	$500	Yours	$400
Fees	700	Parents	200
Books	250	B. Parents	
Supplies	50	Cash	300
Subtotal	$1500	Bank Loans	1000
B. Living		C. Work	
Housing	$850	Summer	
Board	1475	Part-time	
		During	
Personal	75	School Year	
Transportation	300	D. Benefits	
Clothes	225	Social Security	
Entertainment	175	Veteran's	
Subtotal	$3100	Other	
		E. Financial Aid	
Total	$4600	Grants	1200
		Student Loans	600
		Scholarships	400
		F. Other	
		ROTC Pay	900
		Relatives	
		Trusts	
		Total	$5000

III. Summary
   A. Total Resources $5000
   B. Total Expenses   4600
   C. Difference $+400

account statements are issued monthly, the monthly expense budget is convenient for balancing purposes. To establish your monthly expenses, enter the fixed costs first, followed by the discretionary expenses. To arrive at the amounts you're going to allow yourself for discretionary expenses, simply divide your total anticipated costs for those items by the appropriate number of months for which you're budgeting. Once you have compared one month's costs to resources, you can go back and adjust your discretionary income as needed. Chart D illustrates this concept.

CHART D: MONTHLY EXPENDITURE BUDGET

Month: September

Expenses		Resources	
Fixed		My Own	$400
Tuition	$250	Mom and Dad	200
Fees	350	Federal Grant	600
Books	125	Student Loan	300
Dormitory	425	Scholarship	200
Discretionary			
Supplies	35	Bottom Line	
Food	195	Total Resources	1700
Personal	15	Total Expenses	1415
Entertainment	20		
Total	$1415	Balance	$285

This is simply one way to budget for your expenses. Whatever approach you may take, be sure to use a technique that provides you with an ongoing way of tracking your spending and one that accounts for all sorts of expenditures. Above all, once you have developed your plan, stick to it. Be confident in what you've done and disciplined enough to make it work. Your rewards will include the satisfaction of being able to control your destiny in still another way, and being in control of your destiny is proof that you're on your way to becoming an independent, free-thinking adult.

EXERCISE 1

CONSTRUCTING YOUR PERSONAL BUDGET

Determine how much it costs to attend your institution for the academic year. Determine whether you have adequate financial resources to pay for your college education. Using the example in this section as a guide, itemize your expenses and resources for the current year. Then use this information to construct a budget for yourself for the coming year. Once you have your annual budget, use the example in this section to construct a monthly budget for yourself for each month of the *academic* year. Be prepared to share with others what you have learned from this exercise.

I.   ITEMIZE YOUR EXPENSES

Time Period:
A. Educational Expenses
   Tuition $____
   Fees   ____
   Books   ____
   Supplies   ____
      Subtotal $____
B. Living Expenses
   Housing $____
   Board   ____
   Personal   ____
   Transportation   ____
   Clothes   ____
   Entertainment   ____
      Subtotal $____
         Total $____

II. ITEMIZE YOUR RESOURCES

Time Period:
A. Savings
   Yours $____
   Parents   ____
B. Parent Help
   Cash   ____
   Bank Loans   ____
C. Work
   Summer
   Part-time During
      School Year   ____
D. Benefits
   Social Security   ____
   Veteran's   ____
   Other   ____

E. Financial Aid
   Grants   ____
   Scholarships   ____
   Student Loan   ____
F. Other
   ROTC Pay
   Relatives   ____
   Trusts   ____
     Total $____

III. EXPENSE/RESOURCE BUDGET SUMMARY

1. Itemized Expenses
   A. Educational
      Tuition $____
      Fees   ____
      Books   ____
      Supplies   ____
       Subtotal $____
   B. Living
      Housing $____
      Board   ____
      Personal   ____
      Transportation ____
      Clothes   ____
      Entertainment   ____
       Subtotal $____

       Total $____

2. Itemized Resources
   A. Savings
      Yours $____
      Parents   ____
   B. Parents
      Cash   ____
      Bank Loans   ____
   C. Work
      Summer   ____
      Part-time During
        School Year   ____
   D. Benefits
      Social Security   ____
      Veteran's   ____
      Other
   E. Financial Aid
      Grants   ____
      Student Loans   ____
      Scholarships   ____
   F. Other
      ROTC Pay
      Relatives   ____
      Trusts   ____
      Total $____
3. Summary   ____
   A. Total Resources $____
   B. Total Expenses   ____
   C. Difference $____

IV. MONTHLY EXPENDITURE BUDGET

Month: September

Expenses		Resources	
Fixed		My Own	$___
Tuition	$___	Mom and Dad	___
Fees	___	Federal Grant	___
Books	___	Student Loan	___
Dormitory	___	Scholarship	___
Discretionary			
Supplies	___	Bottom Line	
Food	___	Total Resources	___
Personal	___	Total Expenses	___
Entertainment	___		
Total	$___	Balance	$___

■ EXERCISE 2

STEPS IN APPLYING FOR FINANCIAL AID

Visit or contact the financial aid office at your school and find out as much as you can about the types of financial aid programs available. Find out how to apply for financial aid at your school, and familiarize yourself with the application forms.

STEP 14

BECOMING MORE COMFORTABLE WITH YOURSELF AND OTHERS

Two benchmarks of personal growth are your abilities to manage your anxieties and to appreciate your worth as a human being. In this step, we will discuss each of these topics as they affect your success in college.

■ ANXIETY IS NORMAL

The only time we know for sure that people don't feel anxiety is when they're dead! In that context, anxiety is a good thing to have, but it can also become so overwhelming that it may interfere seriously with your ability to perform as you should. Psychologists tell us that a good way to cope with anxiety is to replace it with something that's incompatible with it, something such as relaxation. It's impossible to be tense and relaxed at the same time, and relaxation is a skill you can learn, just as you learn any other skill.

■ WARNING SIGNS OF ANXIETY

Your rate of breathing becomes more rapid and your breaths are shallower. Your heart rate speeds up. You may notice some tension in your muscles at the back of your neck, shoulders, forehead, and perhaps even across your chest. Your hands and feet may become cold and sweaty. You may experience "butterflies" in your stomach, diarrhea, or frequent urination. Your lips dry out, your hands and knees may tremble. Your voice may quiver or even go up an octave.

These are the universal signs of anxiety, caused by an assumed threatening situation, such as speaking in front of a group of people, writing a paper, or studying for an exam. In a threatening situation, we have the urge to do one of two things: either to stand and fight or to run away. Many times, both urges must be suppressed because they would be inappropriate for the situation. Even though you might like to get up and run out of a final exam, it probably would not help your grade if you did, and it's pretty difficult to fight with a piece of paper. So you find that you must often learn to cope with a situation in a way that allows you to face it. This is where learning to manage anxiety can help.

■ MANAGING YOUR ANXIETY

To purposely manage your anxiety, you must first monitor yourself so that you are alert to any signs or symptoms of tension. Once you are aware of these signs, your second goal is to control that anxiety using relaxation techniques to bring your anxiety down to a manageable level. Note that you can never eliminate anxiety totally and it's not even desirable to do so. When athletes go out to perform, they probably won't do a very good job if they're so relaxed that they're just barely awake. On the other hand, if they're so keyed up that they can't contain themselves, they probably won't do well either. Seeking an optimal level of tension is their goal and should be yours.

It is important to know that anxiety is an internally cued response, and therefore can be controlled through the use of imagery. You can simply imagine yourself back in a very tense situation and literally feel the same signs of tension building again in your body. If you imagine a relaxing situation, you should also be able to lower your anxiety to a manageable level.

■ AN EXAMPLE OF ANXIETY LEVELS

Imagine you're sitting in class on the first day of the term and the instructor says, "In this course, we'll have four one-hour examinations." At this point your anxiety level is fairly low. You might assign a higher anxiety "number" to a situation the week before the first exam, when the instructor says, "Now, don't forget next week is our first one-hour exam." Several days before this exam, when you're sitting down to study, your anxiety begins to grow. It's even more pronounced the night before the exam, more as you think about the exam during the night, even more as you wake up and get ready to come to class, more as you walk into the classroom building, into the doorway of the room, into the room, sitting at your desk, looking at other people talking about the exam, hearing the instructor say, "Put your books away," seeing the exams come down the aisle, looking at the exam, seeing that the first question is worth 25 points and not knowing the answer.

We can lump each of these situations together into what we call "test anxiety," yet each individual situation has its own level of tension. It's important to know how differently you feel in each of these situations, and to learn what your anxiety cues are so that you can use them as warning signs.

■ LEVELS OF ANXIETY

Just as anxiety levels build in the example above, so your levels of anxiety grow as you move closer to any potentially tense situation. Being able to identify the earliest warning signs (in the example above, this would be on the first day of class when the professor first announces the four examinations) and working gradually through each of the higher anxiety levels as you practice relaxation techniques—a method in which you associate pleasant thoughts with an anxiety-ridden situation and thereby diffuse the anxiety—you may be able to ultimately reduce your anxieties to a level that will allow you to perform optimally during such events as major examinations.

Ultimately, if you learn relaxation techniques from a qualified counselor, you will be able to progress to what is called a "competency scene." This is where you imagine yourself going through the entire sequence of events, whether it's taking an examination, giving a speech, or whatever. But in this situation, you see yourself doing it the way you really want to do it. When you can complete that process from start to finish—seeing yourself thinking, feeling, speaking, moving exactly the way you want to—calmly, competently, and in a relaxed manner, you have achieved your goal.

Your campus counseling center can provide more information on relaxation techniques, such as self-hypnosis, that can help you weather many of the *normal* "crisis situations" you will encounter during your college days. Seeking help of this sort doesn't label you as abnormal. In fact, the many students who take advantage of personal counseling to help them manage anxieties tend to put these skills to good use throughout their lives.

Once you have learned how to become aware of the very first signs of tension, your goal will be to implement a relaxation process you have learned from a counseling psychologist. A brief version is included in the exercises at the end of this section. You might be surprised after practicing such exercises that your comfort level is much greater than it used to be, and that you simply don't allow yourself to get out of control because you now have skills that you can use anywhere, anytime.

■ ASSERTIVENESS: ANOTHER VALUABLE PERSONAL SKILL

Another valuable skill you can discover at your counseling center is how to stand up for yourself without stepping on others, normally called "assertive behavior." Assertive behavior can also help reduce anxiety simply by giving you more confidence about your thoughts and deeds. More than this, being assertive in your communications will eliminate many of the frustrations and poor relationships with others. To understand what assertive behavior is, we need to define what it is not.

It is not passive behavior. A passive person never speaks up, but uses hints, whines, or "poor me" routines to get his or her way.

It is not aggressive, either. Aggressive people speak in a manner that puts down others. They are demanding and pressuring.

It is not passive-aggressive. An individual expressing this type of behavior promises to be on time and shows up late on purpose.

Nor is assertive behavior any mixture of the above. In fact, none of these attempts at communication is well received by other people, and those who communicate in this way are likely to be rejected or avoided.

■ THE ASSERTIVE POSTURE

Assertive behavior is clear, direct, respectful, responsible communication—verbal and nonverbal. It permits a person to stand up for his or her rights without denying others their rights. If we simply stand up for our rights, with no regard for others, we'll probably come across as aggressive. If we focus exclusively on the rights of another person, ignoring our own rights, we become passive. Attention to our own and others' rights is important in learning to become assertive.

■ PERSONAL AND INTERPERSONAL RIGHTS

Those rights include the right to your own feelings and the right to ask others for what you want or need. To avoid denying others their own rights, we need to be aware of, and consciously acknowledge, the rights of others. Although you have the right to ask a favor, others have the right to refuse to grant it. To stand up assertively for your rights, two conditions must be present that are generally missing from other forms of communication: mutual respect and personal responsibility.

This means: I respect myself and my right to my ideas, feelings, needs, wants, and values. I respect you and your rights to the same. I take responsibility for myself. I don't require you to be responsible for me and for figuring out what I want. I'll figure it out for myself.

■ EXAMPLES OF INAPPROPRIATE BEHAVIORS

Imagine you are serving on a class committee, and Mark isn't doing his share of the work. You are becoming frustrated and worried about the grade you may receive on this project if Mark doesn't come through. The passive approach might be to hint about the deadline, and leave it up to Mark to figure out that you're concerned. This signifies you are not respecting your own needs enough to make them known, and are putting the major responsibility for figuring out what you mean on Mark.

The passive-aggressive approach might be to complain to another committee member. This shows a lack of respect for Mark, the person you should be addressing. This behavior is irresponsible because you probably hope the person you complain to will take the responsibility of telling Mark you are mad at him.

The aggressive approach might be to confront Mark in this manner: "You're messing it up for the rest of us. How can you be so inconsiderate? If you don't get rolling, I'm telling the professor!" This attack ignores Mark's feelings entirely and possibly overlooks circumstances of which you may be unaware. Thus, it is disrespectful.

■ THE ASSERTIVE APPROACH

The assertive approach respects the other person and does not attack him, yet still deals directly with the issues and is responsible enough to express feelings and wishes clearly—in specific words, not by implication or tone of voice.

Thus, the proper answer to the situation above might be, "Mark, I have a problem. Our project is due next week and I'm worried we won't have it ready on time. I had my part ready yesterday, the day we agreed on. I figure you probably have a lot on your mind and may have forgotten we agreed on that date. Still, I'm sort of frustrated and worried we won't have a good project. Would you please pitch in and do your part so we can meet either tomorrow afternoon or noon the next day at the latest? I'd really appreciate it."

Mark may feel embarrassed, but he probably won't feel as if you attacked him. When people are attacked, they defend themselves either by "flight" or "fight." Using flight, they passively comply to your wishes, but resentment builds inside them. Using fight, they openly throw back accusations or fight subversively (passive-aggressive fashion) by getting the work done, but in a slipshod fashion.

When you approach people in a respectful and open manner, chances are they'll hear you more clearly and respond in a more positive manner. You're happier, they're happier. Tension is reduced, and both of you can channel your energies toward getting the job done.

■ RESPECT AND BEING SPECIFIC: KEYS TO ASSERTIVENESS

To speak assertively, you must respect the other person, respect yourself, and be specific in your communications. Respect for the other person doesn't always mean you have to like, admire, or agree with that person. You can dislike someone's behavior and still offer basic human respect. The simple act of saying "Excuse me" as you move through a crowd is one way of respecting the rights of others. Such expressions as "It probably just slipped your mind" show you're willing to respect them even though their behavior has displeased you. Giving the benefit of the doubt is one way to ease the tension in a potential confrontation.

Nonverbal expressions of respect include a clear and unhurried manner of speaking, eye contact with the other person, uncrossed arms to signal openness, and giving others appropriate space so they don't feel crowded or intimidated.

It is equally important to respect yourself and to accept personal responsibility for your feelings and actions. A major way to accomplish this is to say "I feel...," not "You make me feel..."; "I need more time," not "Give me more time." Nonverbal communication of self-respect also includes such things as eye contact and open body movements. Holding your head up instead of lowering it tends to communicate assurance rather than fear. Ending a spoken sentence with a softened, slightly lowered voice shows that you have confidence in what you're saying.

Being specific is the third component of assertive behavior. Specificity means being responsible enough to figure out your views, feelings, and wants, and being able to communicate them as clearly as possible. Instead of saying, "How can you be so inconsiderate?" when a smoker blows smoke in your direction, you can be much more specific and—in the long run—more effective by saying, "I'm having a problem with the smoke from your cigarette. Would you please blow it in another direction?" If you don't like Gloria to keep reading while you're talking to her, don't say, "You don't respect me." Instead, be specific: "I'm uncomfortable when I talk to someone and don't get eye contact, so I'd appreciate it if you'd put down your magazine. It would help a lot."

Managing anxiety and practicing assertive behavior are but two of the ways in which you can actively pursue a program of self-improvement that ultimately leads to greater success in academics, in social situations, in future careers, and in life. To master these and other personal and interpersonal life skills, make a visit to your campus counseling center and find out what they can offer to help you make the most of your college years.

EXERCISE 1

A BRIEF RELAXATION EXERCISE

While this is a highly abridged version of the type of relaxation exercise you can learn at your counseling center, it will nonetheless demonstrate the power of suggestion and the value of imagery in helping you "cool down" your anxiety level in any given situation. Find a comfortable chair, or lie down on your bed or on a soft cushion or carpet and think of a very relaxed scene. This might be a time in your life when you were someplace where you were very calm, very relaxed, and very much at ease. It might help if you closed your eyes and used all five of your senses to experience that situation. For example, you might be at the ocean, walking along in the water up to your knees. As you see yourself walking along, you feel the sand as it gives way beneath your feet. You can also feel the coolness of the water on the lower parts of your legs. You can feel the warmth of the sun on the upper part of your body, and you might even feel the wind as it blows around you. You can smell the salt in the air and, if you were to lick your lips, you could actually taste it. You can hear the sound of the waves as they wash in and out, and perhaps even hear some children playing in the distance. You can see the blue of the ocean, the blue and white of the sky, the white of the sand. And if you put all these together and close your eyes, you can actually feel yourself back there again. Try this with your own "special place," and try to involve all five senses as you do. If you are using this book in a class, discuss the results of such an exercise with others who have done the same thing.

■ EXERCISE 2

DISCOVERING YOUR CAMPUS COUNSELING CENTER

Contact your campus counseling center and find out what's available to you in the areas of relaxation therapy and assertiveness training. Ask about other services offered that might be of interest to freshmen. Report your findings to the class and plan to follow up with an appointment to learn those skills that would help you most.

■ EXERCISE 3

IDENTIFYING BEHAVIORS

Indicate the type of communication in each of the following examples: assertive (AS), passive (P), passive-aggressive (PA), aggressive (AG).

_____ a. Mom indicates she would like her college child to come home each weekend. The student replies: "Mom, I know you love me and want what's best for me. Right now, with studies and the friendships I'm trying to establish, what's best for me is to have most of my weekends here. I won't be coming home except at breaks, but I promise I'll write or call at least once a week. Thanks for understanding."

_____ b. You're asked to do a favor. Your reply: "Are you kidding? Heck, no!"

_____ c. You're a student and need to borrow a classmate's notes. You say: "I don't know what I'm going to do. I missed Dr. Carter's class last Friday and that test of his is next week. Oh, gosh, I know I'm going to screw up. I'll probably flunk."

_____ d. Someone pays you a compliment. You reply: "Thank you. I appreciate your noticing."

_____ e. You're upset with a friend who usually walks in late for meetings. He does it again. You say, "Oh, look. Sam's on time for a change!"

_____ f. You'd like to ask your roommate to play the stereo more softly. You say: "Marie, I don't have any problem with the fact that you enjoy the stereo loud. What I have a problem with is that when I'm here and trying to study, the loud stereo breaks my concentration. When I'm out, do as you like. But, please, when I'm here, keep it lower. I'd appreciate it a lot."

Answers: a. AS   b. AG   c. P   d. AS   e. PA   f. AS

For all of the items above that were not handled assertively, rephrase the response so that it will be assertive.

STEP 15

WHEN YOU FEEL YOUR BEST, YOU DO YOUR BEST

If you will recall our earlier discussion about the holistic development of individuals, you will remember that one important message of this theory is that achievements in one area of development influence many other areas. In this brief discussion of health, exercise, and nutrition, we want to emphasize that—aside from providing you with such benefits as added stamina, a more relaxed attitude, and a general all-around feeling of well-being—good health, proper exercise, and attention to diet can improve the quality of your academic achievements, of your social life, and of many other significant life experiences.

One of the most exciting challenges of being in college is the freedom to create your own personal lifestyle. It's a new experience and a new beginning. As a college student, you have more power and responsibility than ever before, and using your power to help yourself become healthier offers great rewards.

Your health, both physical and emotional, has a great deal to do with your success as a student; and lifestyle habits, the things you do on a day-to-day basis, have everything to do with being, and staying, healthy.

By choosing a lifestyle that includes wholesome foods and vigorous physical activity, you take a giant step toward health, well-being, and success. You can be vigorously alive, feel great, and be alert and prepared for many things. You can have sufficient energy, not only for meeting the daily demands of classroom assignments, but also for the fun, social events, and personal relationships that enhance college life.

These years can well be the perfect time to establish lifetime patterns that can enhance the quality, and perhaps the quantity, of your entire life.

Let's look, then, at the difference a healthy lifestyle can make during your college years.

■ IS FATIGUE NORMAL?

Fatigue can be caused by a number of things, among them over-work and overexertion. But many college students experience fatigue for other reasons: lack of rest, not eating the proper foods, and not getting the proper exercise. Unfortunately, too many col-lege students accept feeling tired and sluggish as "normal." If you wake up every morning feeling tired and irritable, you may not realize that others look forward to morning as the best part of the day. They're raring to go each morning and have energy to spare and a genuine zest for life. If you asked them how they managed to feel this way, chances are it would have something to do with exercise, rest, and nutrition.

We have already established in the previous section that you're important enough to start doing something about anxiety and misleading communications to others. Taking care of your body falls into the same category. In fact, many people believe in a "mind-body connection," which means, simply, that when your body is in good shape, your mind tends to function more fluidly, and you feel better emotionally, too.

Perhaps it has something to do with the nourishment your brain cells receive from your healthy body; whatever the reason, a num-ber of books have been written to support the theory that a healthy body nurtures a healthy mind, and vice-versa.

■ EXCUSES ARE EASY TO COME BY

You don't have time to exercise. Running is boring. It's impossible to eat properly on your schedule. The campus snack bar serves nothing but junk food. Studying late eats into your sleeping hours. There just aren't enough hours in the day to do all these things, attend classes and study, and enjoy life, too.

Those who do run and watch their diet offer answers that contradict those excuses. Many people who have gotten into the habit of running, walking, or swimming three times a week or more claim they are more productive after exercising than before. "I spend about 90 minutes swimming, showering, dressing, and having lunch," says a professor. "When I get back to my desk, I feel recharged, and my mind actually seems to work faster than ever. I can't believe how much work I can plow through in one afternoon when most people are experiencing their energy low point of the day."

Or listen to a student who found she could eat properly, even in the university cafeteria: "I choose salads from the salad bar, broiled rather than fried foods; I take advantage of all the fresh cooked vegetables they serve. Sometimes I just load up on vegetables and skip the meat. Other times, I look for chicken or turkey or fish instead of beef."

■ THE TIME TO BEGIN IS NOW

Although the leading causes of death in our country—heart disease, cancer, stroke, and diabetes—usually manifest themselves in middle age, they often are attributed to diet and exercise habits that began much earlier in life. Millions of Americans are malnourished, not in the traditional sense, but in the form of overconsumption of highly processed "junk foods" that are loaded with sugar, salt, and fat. Unfortunately, college students are major consumers of junk foods.

The average college student consumes approximately 126 pounds of sugar a year and two to five times more salt than is necessary for the body to function. As much as 40 percent of his daily caloric intake comes from fats. With processed convenience foods readily available, it takes awareness and extra effort to choose foods that are wholesome.

■ EATING BETTER

Although the nutritionist at your campus health center can provide much more detailed information than is possible on these pages, we offer five basic rules for improving the quality of your eating.

1. Increase consumption of fruits, vegetables, and whole grains. Of the foods you eat daily, the greatest number of calories (50 to 60 percent) should come from these sources. These foods are classified as complex carbohydrates (refined sugars are not included).

2. Reduce intake of fats and foods high in fats. This can mean cutting down on the amount of red meat consumed (and that includes hamburgers), substituting more poultry and fish, and having meatless days several times a week. Since fat is more concentrated in calories, foods that are high in fat content tend to have more calories, ounce for ounce, than low-fat foods.

3. Reduce cholesterol intake to 300 mg daily. Go easy on meats (especially fatty red meats and pork), shellfish (shrimp, lobster), and eggs. Substitute skim milk or low-fat milk for whole milk. One egg has almost 300 mg of cholesterol, so it may be wise to have no more than three eggs a week.

4. Decrease consumption of sugar and foods high in sugar. Approximately 80 percent of the sugar we eat is hidden in processed foods. Get into the label-reading habit. Ingredients are listed according to their percentage within the product. If sugar is listed first in the ingredients list, this means the product has more sugar than anything else.

5. Reduce salt consumption. Limiting salty snack items and most fast foods will go far in reducing salt intake. Experiment with other seasonings and spices, such as lemon, pepper, and orega-

no. Read labels. Look for the words "soda" and "sodium" and the
symbol "Na" on the labels (sodium bicarbonate, monosodium
glutamate, sodium benzoate, and so on).

On campus, keep fresh fruit in your room for snacks. Drink fruit
juice, skim milk, or water with meals rather than sodas. Choose
fresh fruits over pastries for desserts, and seek out restaurants that
have salad bars.

■ STARTING AN EXERCISE PROGRAM

Many people who give up exercise after making a start are guilty of
working too hard at it and missing out on the fun. The proper way
to begin a program is to join a group in which someone who knows
exercise can get you started in the proper way. If you experience
muscle aches and twinges of joint pain during the first week, that's
normal. Such discomforts should disappear shortly.

■ CHOOSING THE BEST EXERCISE

The best exercise is one you do consistently. For most of us, that
means it should be relatively inexpensive, convenient, and enjoyable. It should also be steady, sustained, and vigorous activity. The
ideal exercise conditions your muscles and cardiovascular system
and makes you physically fit, but is not overly strenuous. Constant
and rhythmic activities such as walking, jogging or running,
swimming, aerobic dancing, racquetball, cycling, and cross-country
skiing are best.

■ THE BENEFITS OF EXERCISE

Exercise can make you feel fantastic! More specifically, proper and
regular exercise can reduce your heart rate and blood pressure,
increase your heart size and cardiac work capacity, increase heart-
pumping efficiency, increase oxygen-carrying ability of the blood,
increase respiratory efficiency, reduce body weight and percent of
body fat, suppress appetite, burn up stored fat tissue, and prevent
adult-onset diabetes.

Exercising also promotes a feeling of well-being, has a tranquilizing effect, can help prevent depression, promotes feelings of self-control, self-confidence, and improved body image, and even promotes sound sleep.

The first step is always the hardest, but the rewards of being physically fit and active can greatly outweigh your initial effort.

■ EXERCISE 1
BREAKING THE PATTERN

For just one week, follow the suggestions for eating properly in this section of the book. This means that for one week, you will avoid junk foods, hamburgers, fatty foods, rich desserts, salt, and sugar. Even though it takes a special effort, be deliberate in your choices of foods. Include salads, chicken, turkey, fish, broiled rather than fried foods, plenty of fresh and cooked vegetables, and fresh fruits. Use skim milk and have it with a tasty, whole-grain cereal. Cut down on consumption of eggs, gravies, heavy sauces, and milkshakes. At the end of the week, write a paper discussing the experience, whether or not you intend to go back to your old eating habits, and why.

■ EXERCISE 2
BREAKING INTO AN EXERCISE ROUTINE

Contact the physical education center at your campus and ask them to put you in touch with an expert on exercise. Meet with this person and have him or her recommend an exercise program for you. Then take whatever steps are necessary to begin this program. If you would prefer swimming to running, for example, but have never learned to swim, ask about swimming lessons at your college. Try to exercise at least three times a week for limited periods (30 minutes or so). After three weeks, reflect on the way you feel, and on whether or not you intend to keep up with such a program.

STEP 16

ALCOHOL, DRUGS, AND THE ISSUE OF RESPONSIBILITY

To make things clear at the start of this section, we are not about to use these pages to preach to you about the evils of alcohol and other drugs. In the first place, we're professors, not preachers. In the second place, we know full well that attempting to fill you with warnings and admonitions about the subject may only fall on deaf ears.

Now that we've spoken openly, we need to ask that you return the favor by reading this with an open mind, and avoid making assumptions until you've heard us out. Fair enough?

For many years, colleges and universities have offered programs on alcohol and drug education for students, but recent times have added a new wrinkle to the problem, as states from South Carolina to Oregon raise their legal drinking ages to 21. This means, quite frankly, that the majority of college-age students are prohibited by law from purchasing alcoholic beverages or paying others to purchase such beverages for them. In other words, if you are caught in such a situation, you may be guilty of a misdemeanor.

As for other drugs, nothing has changed regarding their legality. In a word, they're not legal. More importantly, drugs such as marijuana, heroin, cocaine, and crack have devastated the lives of many, young and old, in recent years. If you don't know by now of the dangers of using such drugs, we recommend an immediate visit to your campus alcohol and drug center.

Clearly, such drugs are both dangerous and destructive. As for alcohol, the issues are not so clearly drawn. If you lived in a vacuum, you might assume that such laws would eliminate any drinking problems for college students. But you and we know better, of course. When the federal government instituted Prohibition in the early part of this century, people circumvented the law by finding illegal methods for manufacturing and consuming alcohol until, during the 1930s, the government realized it could not legislate against an entrenched social practice, and repealed Prohibition.

Without taking an advocacy position on this controversial topic, we merely want to register our concern that the prohibition of drinking by individuals under the age of 21 may lead to the same sort of covert consumption of alcohol among college students. When something is illegal, it tends to become more appealing, and alcohol is certainly no exception to this rule. All this points to the fact that, although many college students shouldn't, by law, be drinking, the evidence is very much to the contrary. Therefore, alcohol education remains a vital topic on college campuses—not in the form of arguments against drinking, but rather as reasoned and responsible commentary on the effects of drinking and a reminder that, as with other things in your life at this stage, the decision to drink or how much to drink should be *your* decision, not something you do because others happen to be doing it.

College is traditionally a time for experimenting and testing your limits, and one option that will require some important decisions is the use of alcohol or other drugs. The primary drug of abuse among today's college and high school students is alcohol. The latest research shows that people are beginning to drink much earlier (at age 16 or less) than previously, so that by the time they reach college, their drinking habits may be firmly established.

■ WHY DO PEOPLE DRINK?

"Everyone else is doing it" is the answer you most often hear. If drinking is part of your peer group's activity, it becomes one of the things you share with them, another way to strengthen the bond between them and you. If the drinking is kept in perspective and not given undue importance, it's simply a part of your shared activity. If it becomes the most important issue in the group, however, trouble can result. In other words, if the amount you drink is the only measure of success in your group, you may want to question why the group exists at all. You will probably also discover that any attempt to become singled out as "a really good drinker" may result in problems with the more important aspects of your college experience. If you have already chosen to drink before you get to college, deciding when to drink and how to drink still remain vital issues of concern for you.

■ WHEN SHOULD I DRINK?

It is generally accepted that people generally drink for relaxation or to enjoy a social event. This may be all well and good, provided that you consume only a reasonable amount and that such behavior does not interfere with the more important events in your life. If a mid-term exam is coming up tomorrow, it wouldn't make much sense to spend the night before drinking and partying, would it? On the other hand, if you finish the work week and it's time to relax, that may be the ideal time to socialize and enjoy a reasonable amount of alcohol with friends.

Quite often, the decision to drink at a certain time stems not from a suggestion or invitation by others, but has to do with how you feel at the time. It's certainly normal to be down sometimes, and that in itself is no reason to panic or worry about yourself. But sometimes you can feel there's no way to get rid of bad feelings unless you drink. After all, relaxing with a couple of friends and a few beers is one way to feel better. Once more, that may not be a bad idea, unless you begin to rely on alcohol instead of looking for more productive ways to deal with problems.

When people rely on alcohol or drugs to relieve their bad feelings about problems, the only things that change, temporarily, are the feelings. Unfortunately, the problems are still there when you sober up and you find you haven't really solved the major issue at all.

A more realistic solution might be to determine the source of the problem and address it directly. If you don't understand much of what a professor says in class, and this has you worried about your grade, the best thing to do is to go to the professor and talk about it. It's far less risky to relax over a few drinks and hope the problem will not seem as important later. The fallacy in this logic is that the problem doesn't change until you take steps to change it.

So the question of when to drink becomes a matter of choosing a time or event that (a) won't have a negative effect on more important matters in your life and (b) is appropriate for all parties involved (you probably wouldn't choose to have a few beers during a conference with your professor, even if it were Friday afternoon and you were walking straight back to your dorm afterwards!).

Another occasion for drinking, and one that enhances the experience in a different way, is when you are enjoying a meal. Drinking wine with a meal, for example, often helps you enjoy subtle differences in the taste and smell of food. If you drink leisurely with meals, you're very likely to enjoy both the drink and the food. If you drink too much or too quickly, your senses become dulled, and you're likely to miss the enjoyment of good food altogether.

■ HOW MUCH TO DRINK

We have already mentioned that most drinking occurs in a social setting with other people. Used in a responsible way, alcohol can enhance and add to the enjoyment of many social events. In terms of escaping everyday stress, socializing with friends, laughing, and sharing good feelings are probably very healthy things to do. When you add a reasonable amount of alcohol to the situation, you can probably relax even more thoroughly, and there's a simple reason for that.

Any alcohol you ingest is absorbed quickly and directly into your bloodstream through the stomach wall and small intestine. As soon as it's in the bloodstream, it begins to circulate and goes almost immediately to the brain, particularly the area governing your judgment, inhibitions, and self-control.

With a reasonable amount of alcohol, this causes you to feel relaxed, more talkative, and consequently more sociable. Unfortunately, many people feel that if one drink makes them feel that
good, two are better, and four are surely better than two.

In actuality, to maintain this relaxed feeling requires less than one
drink per hour. This means one beer, one mixed drink, or one
5-ounce glass of wine, since they all contain the same amount of
alcohol. Your body can only rid itself of 1 to 1 1/4 ounces of alcohol
per hour, and you can maintain your relaxed feeling by limiting
your drinking to this amount for a full hour.

■ HOW YOU DRINK

The way you choose to drink is generally determined by what you
want to get out of the situation. If you want to be sociable and
relaxed, one drink an hour is enough to help you do that. In
reminiscing about the good times, you'll find that you and others
generally remember the best times as those where drinking was
not the focus of the event, but only a part of the reason for being
there. The real emphasis was on being with a great group of
people, and enjoying their company as well as perhaps good music
and good food in a relaxing and inviting atmosphere. When you
drink too much, it's difficult to remember much about the evening
at all. Much of the excessive drinking that occurs among college
students may be the result of thinking that others expect this of you.
Try spending your time instead discovering what really makes a
party memorable.

■ RESPONSIBLE DRINKING

The concept of responsible drinking is a relatively new one on
college campuses. It's based on the assumption that you can't
legislate against drinking, and that drinking in moderation is
respectable, responsible, and pleasurable. For this reason, it
appears to make sense to provide facts about alcohol in an un-
biased manner so that you can make educated decisions about
using or not using it.

In the past, educators attempted to use scare tactics, such as stories about people whose lives were destroyed by alcohol addiction. While many of these stories were frightening, they also served to arouse the curiosity of many students about this "forbidden fruit." The more mature high school students simply ignored this approach.

The next approach consisted of films of accidents and injuries resulting from excessive drinking. While effectively scary, the films were often so horrible that people blocked them out and thereby ignored the obvious message. "It couldn't happen to me," was a typical response.

Responsible drinking emphasizes the presentation of clear facts about the effects of alcohol and drugs. A major difference in this approach from its predecessors is that responsible drinking never assumes that something evil is going to happen to you should you decide to drink. We generally respond to such admonitions in a negative and angry manner, so responsible drinking tactics simply present the facts and ask you to think about your decision.

■ SO HERE ARE THE FACTS

One of the very first things alcohol affects is your ability to make sound judgments. It also affects your level of inhibition. After the first few drinks, your judgment is affected, and with each additional drink, other things begin to happen. You feel off-balance, and your words may become slurred. Your reaction time slows down, and your vision and coordination become subnormal. Add to these effects a lack of inhibition, and you may begin doing things like dancing with a lampshade on your head, careening into people and furniture, and acting generally like a total idiot.

With your judgment impaired, it's no wonder you may feel (a) it's time to head for home and (b) you're perfectly capable of driving a car. The fact is, at a blood alcohol level of 0.10, you are seven times more likely to have an accident than if you were sober. Your coordination, depth perception, reaction time, judgment, and inhibitions have been considerably altered by your excessive consumption of alcoholic beverages.

The facts are alarming. In a recent year, 50,000 people were killed on the road, and 50 percent of these accidents were caused by a driver who had been drinking. The evidence suggests that the use of drugs can impair a driver's abilities as much as drinking can. You've heard this a hundred times if you've heard it at all, but the fact remains that you shouldn't drink if you're driving, and if you've been drinking, you shouldn't drive.

■ ALCOHOL, DRINKING, AND THE LAW

You should also know that every state now has an Implied Consent Law. This means that by accepting a driver's license, you agree that you will take a breathalyzer test, if requested, by an officer who has reason to ask you to do so. Refusal to do this can cause your license to be revoked for up to 90 days or more, and when you go to court you may still be charged with driving under the influence.

Now think about it. If you lose your right to drive, even temporarily, it's going to have a major impact on your life. If you work, this creates other problems. Many states also require you to attend a training program if you are charged with DUI (drinking under the influence), and you go at your expense, over and above any fines assessed in court.

Your insurance rates can be raised up to three or even five times their normal rate if you are so charged, and can remain high for as long as three years. So aside from the extreme danger to yourself and others that drunk driving creates, it can be a very expensive matter, even if you don't serve a jail term, which is possible.

It's much safer—and smarter—to plan ahead. If you know you're going to drink, find a driver who will not get drunk and will get everyone home safely. If this isn't possible, stay where you are. Most everyone has a floor space where you can sleep. If you can't stay, call a cab or a friend, and get them to take you home. Listen to your friends, too. If they tell you that you're too drunk to drive, listen to them.

■ ADDICTIONS TO ALCOHOL AND OTHER DRUGS

While the incidence of full-blown addiction occurs only in a small number of students while they're in college, it does happen to about 5 percent of the population. If you develop habits of heavy drinking and/or drug use in college, they could stay with you in later life. The average American alcoholic is difficult to identify, since most are employed, married, have families, and generally function normally in society. Such people become much more like our stereotypes of alcoholics when their addiction causes them to lose their jobs, separate from their families, and get kicked out of their homes into the streets.

Certain behaviors can indicate the presence of a possible problem: (1) drinking when there's a good reason to stay sober; (2) getting into fights or being thrown out of places because of drinking; (3) getting into trouble with the law because of drinking; (4) having accidents and being injured because of drinking; (5) drinking alone and/or needing a drink in the morning; (6) having shaking hands the morning after; (7) not being able to remember what happened the night before; and (8) being told by a doctor that drinking is affecting your health.

Many of these things can happen to anyone once, and perhaps twice, but if they become regular occurrences, you are looking at a serious problem.

■ GETTING HELP

At times, even the most well-adjusted person may have difficulties dealing with life, and may benefit from the help others have to offer. Here is where you might begin to look on campus for such help:

■ *Friends and Fellow Students.* Talking to someone like yourself can be a rewarding experience. You'll probably find out that most people feel the way you do, and that you can help one another solve problems.

■ *Hall Advisors and Residence Directors.* If you live in a residence hall, check in with this person. He or she is usually an upperclass student who knows how to help you or can put you in touch with other helping resources on campus.

■ *Professors and Academic Advisors.* While they're more inclined to discuss your academic problems than your personal ones, the line between the two is often a fine one, and you may be surprised to discover how empathetic they can be when you need help.

■ *Counseling Centers and Chaplain's Offices.* These professional counselors offer a wide variety of services to students experiencing problems.

That's what we have to say about drinking. Now it's up to you to make the decisions. To drink or not. When to drink. How to drink. How much to drink. Many people who drink socially know how to enjoy alcohol without endangering themselves or others. It's not as easy as it may seem, but with a little practice, a little common sense, and some help from caring friends, you can find a sensible and responsible way to handle these choices. That's what you should be doing. What you shouldn't do is be swayed by others who imply that drinking is the only path to acceptance by your peers. Believe us, it just ain't so.

■ EXERCISE 1

ALCOHOL. FACTS VS. MYTHS.

Take this brief quiz. Then, check the correct answers against yours and discuss the reactions to the answers and other information in this section with other members of your class. How misinformed were you and they about drinking? How has the information in this section changed your views about drinking?

1. People do things when they are drunk that they would never do when sober. True or False?

2. About what percentage of adults in America drinks alcoholic beverages? a. 95 percent   b. 70 percent   c. 50 percent   d. 33 percent

3. Alcohol is a stimulant. True or False?

4. Fifteen percent of all people killed in drunk driving accidents are in their teens. True or False?

5. How many alcoholics are estimated to be in the United States? a. 500,000   b. 5–6 million   c. 9–10 million   d. 15 million

6. Most people can judge when they are too drunk to drive. True or False?

7. In most states, the blood alcohol level at which you are legally drunk is: a. 0.05   b. 0.10   c. 0.12   d. 0.15

8. Americans spend as much on alcohol as they do on education. True or False?

9. Best estimates indicate that ___ percent of all highway fatalities are alcohol related.

10. Black coffee, walking, or cold showers will sober up a drunk faster. True or False?

11. A large person will sober up more quickly than a small person. True or False?

12. Alcohol is an aphrodisiac. True or False?

13. Which has the greatest amount of alcohol in it? a. one drink mixed with 80-proof liquor   b. one 4-ounce glass of 12 percent wine   c. one 12-ounce beer   d. all have the same

14. A person may overdose on alcohol just as with other drugs. True or False?

15. Certain behaviors can serve as warnings to tell a person that he or she may have a drinking problem. How many can you name?

Answers

1. True. Inhibitions are lowered by drinking, giving us "permission" to do things we might be too shy or smart to do when sober.

2. b. 70 percent.

3. False. Many feel it's a stimulant because it lowers inhibitions, and because it relaxes or loosens us up. In reality, alcohol is a depressant.

4. False. The figure is approximately 60 percent.

5. c. 9–10 million. These are alcoholics, not just heavy drinkers.

6. False. Most people are horrible judges of this. As the brain is more affected by drinking, we are less able to judge our level of debilitation.

7. b. 0.10. You can, however, be arrested and charged with DUI with a blood alcohol level as low as 0.05 if the officer determines that you cannot function reponsibly.

8. False. They spend about twice as much on drinking.

9. c. 50 percent. This is approximately 25,000 people per year.

10. False. All you get is a wide-awake drunk. The body processes 1 to 1 1/4 ounces of alcohol out of your body per hour. Time is the only thing that will sober you up.

11. False. We all sober up at the same rate. A large person may need to drink more than a small one to get to the same level of intoxication, however.

12. False. It lowers inhibitions and makes us more willing to take risks and do things we might not otherwise do, but it also lowers sensitivity and at legally drunk levels can impair sexual performance, especially among males.

13. d. All have the same amount of real alcohol in them, 1 to 1 1/2 ounces.

14. True. When you pass out (not black out), the body is going to sleep so that no more alcohol can be put into it.

15. Here are twelve signals to watch out for:
    1. Drinking when there is a good reason not to, or getting drunk when there is good reason not to.
    2. Having accidents or injuring yourself because of drinking.

3. Missing classes or appointments because of drinking.
4. Getting into fights because of drinking.
5. Being asked to leave a bar or party because of drinking.
6. Blackouts: When you can't remember what happened when you were drinking, even though you continued to function during that time.
7. Getting into trouble with the law because of drinking.
8. Needing a drink to "get you going" in the morning.
9. Using money for drinking that should have been used for something else.
10. Having shaky hands the next morning.
11. Being told by a doctor that drinking is affecting your health.
12. Feeling the effects of drinking in class or on the job.

STEP 17

MAKING IT FEEL LIKE HOME

For many of you attending college, you are about to experience still another major change in your lifestyle. For the first time in your lives, many of you will be living away from your families for an extended period of time. Actually, you have only three choices in terms of where to live while attending college. If your college happens to be in or near your hometown, you may decide to remain at home. Your second choice would be to move into one of the on-campus dormitories, while a third choice would be to live off-campus with friends or alone.

Because your total development—not simply your academic progress—is critical during this period, it's essential to know just what each of these options offers, especially when you realize that you will probably spend more waking hours where you live than anywhere else. If you choose to live away from your family home, or are forced to because your college is far from your hometown, you will be facing new experiences, new situations, and new people with whom you'll be living. Being able to adjust to this new situation comfortably can have a great influence on how well you perform academically, as well as how much you enjoy the total college experience.

So let's look at your three options in detail, and let you determine which might be most suitable for you.

■ LIVING ON CAMPUS

Residence halls (dormitories) are a product of the European influence on higher education. American colleges built residence halls modeled on those of Cambridge and Oxford Universities in England in an attempt to involve students more completely in the academic life of the college, and to allow students to meet with, learn from, and live with faculty members. The interest in fraternity and sorority houses grew from this concept to answer a need for students who wanted both a place to live and membership in an organization.

Because students spend much of their time in residence halls, colleges place great importance on residence hall activities to provide residents with additional growth experiences. These might include informal coffees with faculty, informal "classes" taught by residents to one another on a variety of skills and interests, regular classes taught in your dorm, intramural athletic competitions, social events, seminars by faculty and staff or professionals from business and industry, and other activities suggested by the residents themselves.

■ CHARACTERISTICS OF CAMPUS LIVING

Living on campus may cause you to adjust your habits to some degree. Although your residence hall counselor may be around to supervise, he or she probably won't check to see that you're in bed at a respectable hour, or that you devote sufficient time to your studies. In most cases, you'll be sharing the room with one or more people who may come from different backgrounds. Living in a residence hall provides residents with a chance to learn and study together, to explore new frontiers of thinking, and to learn about many lifestyles that may be different than yours. Close friendships often develop in this setting; some are maintained for life.

■ OTHER RESIDENCE HALL OPTIONS

Theme halls and coed dorms are options you may wish to consider if your choice is to live on campus. Theme halls or theme floors allow residents with special interests to live together. Examples might be language houses (Spanish, German, French, etc.), honors halls, creative arts halls, history halls, or engineering halls. Coeducational halls are also becoming commonplace on many college campuses, with males on one floor, females on the other. Often, males and females may live next door to one another in apartment-like settings. Although such living arrangements have been sensationalized in the press on occasion, the truth is that coeducational living generally allows men and women to develop a healthy respect for the opposite sex. Instead of the wild partying many expect, such dorms tend to foster friendships as individuals blossom in a real-world environment.

■ LIVING AT HOME

Surprisingly, if you choose to live at home, or must do so for financial reasons, you will find that you have to make as many adjustments in your lifestyle as the student who moves away from home.

First, your class schedule will vary from day to day. This and your commitments to other activities on campus may mean you won't be able to join the family for dinner each evening. If you have younger brothers or sisters at home, they may need to understand that you need quiet time for studying on a regular basis, now that you're in college. Other demands of academic work may cause you to miss family outings, and can strain the family relationship.

You can reduce this conflict by explaining your situation to the rest of your family as early as possible. It may help to talk with friends who are facing the same situation for suggestions on smoothing over any bad feelings about your new lifestyle. You might also consider making friends with residence hall students to become acquainted with their lifestyles. This can also provide an opportunity to learn what it's like to live away from home.

■ LIVING WITH FRIENDS

Your third option, living off-campus with friends, involves a different set of adjustments and added responsibilities. For starters, household chores such as cooking, cleaning, and laundry will have to be shared in some manner that is agreeable to all residents of your house or apartment. Financing the venture will require some sort of budget. You'll need to set aside money for rent, food, utilities, telephone, cleaning supplies, and so forth. You may often find that you will have to readjust the budget periodically because bills ran higher than anticipated.

Living off-campus is the most independent lifestyle of the three. No one will be supervising you, and the demands on your time will be greater because of the household tasks that must be completed. This is a good reason to budget your time carefully, to allow for study and relaxation. This living arrangement can be a worthwhile and fulfilling experience as long as it's handled properly by all parties involved, and can also be a great deal of fun.

■ SPECIAL SITUATIONS

If you're living at home as a husband or wife, you will need to make a different sort of adjustment. Budgeting time for study will be extremely important. The parent attending college will need to work out a schedule to cope with both college and children's demands, and both parents will need to agree on priorities.

If you must hold down a job while in college, budgeting your time is also extremely important. By working, you cut down on the number of hours available for other activities, such as studying. In both of these special situations, careful planning and an early understanding by all parties concerned can avoid conflicts.

■ GOING HOME AGAIN

If you find yourself living away from home, you'll probably learn to become independent and develop as an individual. As a result, you may have other adjustments to make whenever you return home. You leave home as a teenager, and each time you return, you're more of an adult.

There's no need to be concerned about such changes, because they're healthy. But you will need to exercise tact and diplomacy with parents. Surely your patience will be tried if they try to treat you as a teenager; but remember, that's what you were like when they last saw you! With patience and understanding, you and your parents can establish a warm, new adult-to-adult relationship.

■ WHICH SHALL IT BE?

Choosing a residence hall will allow you to take part in activities, programs, projects, and learning experiences with a group of people who live in your area. Being right on campus makes it easy to get to classes, to the PE center, the library, the student union, and other areas where students tend to congregate. Living with friends provides an opportunity to become responsible for your own living quarters, to learn to live on a household budget, and to simulate an adult living experience. Living at home reduces your financial outlay, may offer you the privacy you need, and keeps you in touch with the family on a regular basis.

Each option has its benefits and drawbacks, and each one is probably right for different individuals. Another option you have is to vary your options from year to year. If you live at home one year, you may wish to move on campus the following year. You might choose to move from residence hall to sorority or fraternity house, from parent's home to an apartment with friends, and so on. There's no ideal setting for everyone, except that any living environment should provide you with a setting that allows for quiet study, chances to make friends and socialize, and the opportunity to make the most of your college years.

■ EXERCISE 1

COMPARING LIVING OPTIONS

Form a group of three students. Each student should keep a list of
the advantages and disadvantages of living in one of the three
situations discussed in this section. When you have completed your
lists, discuss them and try to arrive at a description of the type of
student who might be happiest (or unhappiest) living in each of the
situations.

■ EXERCISE 2

LEARNING ABOUT OTHER LIFESTYLES

Interview two students who have chosen different living options
than you have chosen. Find out what they have to say about the
advantages and disadvantages of their living arrangements, and ask
why they chose this option and whether they will choose it again.

STEP 18

AVOIDING THAT LEFT-OUT FEELING. ACTIVITIES AND LEADERSHIP.

Throughout this book, we have stressed that education and personal development occur beyond the classroom during the years you spend in college. Nothing could document this fact more thoroughly than the areas we're about to explore: extracurricular activities and student leadership within those activities.

We also want to stress that years of research indicate that freshmen who join activities are more likely to become sophomores, something we're sure you want to be!

Regardless of the size of the college or university you attend, you will soon discover a commitment to student activities on campus. You may find yourself involved in one-on-one activities, such as competing in a billiards tournament or attending a film or lecture on campus. You may join a small group activity, such as participating in a theatrical performance or joining a student newspaper staff. Or you may find yourself in a large campus group, such as student government, a social fraternity or sorority, or the campus choir.

Despite the level of involvement you choose, dozens of opportunities exist. Let's explore some of the major areas available to you.

■ INTRAMURAL AND RECREATIONAL SPORTS

Whether it involves an individual or team sport and is co-rec, all-male, or all-female, the opportunity is there. Though the events—which may include football, basketball, water polo, or a 6.2

mile run—are certainly competitive, your enthusiasm and willingness to learn are equally important. You may also find various sport clubs on your campus—a backpacking club, a flying club, a parachuting club, for example—which not only provide an opportunity to know people with similar interests, but also offer a chance to develop lifelong skills.

■ STUDENT ORGANIZATIONS

The many student organizations on your campus usually fall within the broad boundaries of social, religious, academic, political, or service organizations, and might include such groups as:

- Karate Club
- Greek fraternities
- College Republicans
- Christian Fellowship
- Finance Club
- Chess Club
- Sailing Club
- Student newspaper
- Association of Afro-American Students
- Graduate Women's Association
- Bowling League
- Amnesty International
- PE Majors Club
- Student Bar Association

Social organizations traditionally have been popular because they offer the chance to work and relax with people who share common interests. The comfort of a religious organization offers many students this same sort of camaraderie. In recent years, academic-related student organizations have become popular with students. For a business major interested in a marketing career, joining the student marketing club offers the advantage of hearing guest speakers from industry with others who share your interests. Such clubs often promote social activities as well. Since many faculty participate in such activities, this is also a good way to become more friendly with them, and may lead to recommendations for jobs as you approach graduation.

■ STUDENT UNION

Almost every college union has a group of committees for providing students with a well-rounded set of programs. Such committees may include those that plan lectures, cultural series, films, concerts, short courses, and travel programs. These committees plan, produce, and evaluate such program areas, and need many student volunteers. Working on such a team can provide you with firsthand experience in budgeting, publicity, and leadership skills as you learn to get along with and lead others. You can use such experience to complement your academic major, or to find out about a totally new field.

■ STUDENT MEDIA

Your campus newspaper, yearbook, and radio station report on campus events and provide entertainment. As a newspaper reporter, you can learn to interview, write a story, and work your way to an editorship. You may also want to use your skills in photography, or gain sales experience as an advertising representative and earn income as well. Your radio station can offer you the chance to become a disc jockey, news reporter, or program director.

■ FRATERNITIES, SORORITIES. MYTHS AND REALITIES.

For many students, the question of whether or not to pledge a Greek social organization is a casual one. For others, it can assume the importance of life itself, while for a third group it is to be avoided at all costs. Regardless of how you may feel, Greek organizations offer still another opportunity for friendship and social interaction, and are still another place in which to develop leadership skills. Membership in a fraternity or sorority is both an opportunity and a responsibility. You have the opportunity to live in the fraternity or sorority house and enjoy the benefits of communal living with friends. You can get involved in formal dances, mixers with other chapters, or playing on an intramural team. Membership is also a responsibility requiring your time, energy, and enthusiasm. It also requires your financial support.

Dues vary widely from chapter to chapter and from campus to campus, but a general fee of $200 to $500 per year, not including room and board, can be expected. If you consider a fraternity or sorority, you should determine what it will cost and how you will be able to meet those costs for all four years of typical undergraduate membership. If you decide to join a Greek organization, remember to visit a number of groups and seek a group of people you enjoy being with and whom you like and respect.

■ DEVELOPING LEADERSHIP SKILLS

One of the most exciting opportunities of belonging to any student organization is the opportunity to become a leader of that group. Most of us, whether we realize it or not, harbor a secret desire to be a leader. The reasons many of us never realize this ambition are varied, but they usually have to do with not being able to justify the added time and energy the task will require. Viewed another way, however, taking the time to learn leadership skills can be as enriching an experience as pursuing your academic subjects.

As a student leader, you'll learn how to motivate others, resolve conflicts, communicate your ideas to others, administer praise and criticism tactfully, run a meeting, accept and delegate responsibility, manage committees, make decisions, solve problems, manage projects, plan and organize, recruit volunteers, and more. You'll learn about time management, financial management, and the important skills of dealing with success and failure. You'll find it easier to deal with shyness and to cope with stress. You'll feel better about yourself as you become more aware of your strengths and limitations. These are valuable life skills which will help you long after your college years are over. Student leaders also tend to be more socially oriented and more popular—two more good reasons to seek a leadership position in your organization. What we're suggesting is that the payoffs far outweigh the risk and time commitments of leadership.

■ PREPARING FOR LEADERSHIP

The truth is, no student leader is adequately prepared for his or her first or second or subsequent leadership position, just as you aren't ready to pass the final exam on the first day of class. Furthermore, if you don't do something well, you become more highly motivated to become accomplished at it. Even though assuming leadership may make you feel inadequate, uncomfortable, or stressed, remember that it's quite normal to feel this way.

Once you're convinced of the benefits of leadership, the next step is to join a club or organization early in your college career. Once involved, stay involved. Accept responsibilities for even minor assignments such as hanging posters, sitting at a voting booth, or arranging the cleanup committee for a major activity. Work your way up gradually to major tasks, trying leadership skills you've seen model leaders use. Never hesitate to ask for the advice of those who are older, wiser, and more experienced than you. Once you taste the thrill of leadership, you'll discover yourself working harder to become the best leader you can be. At the same time, as you will soon realize, you'll also find yourself accomplishing more—and feeling better about those accomplishments—in many walks of life.

■ BENEFITS OF STUDENT ACTIVITIES

Besides providing a valuable practical experience, your involvement in student activities, as we have already suggested, offers many other significant benefits. You'll meet students with similar interests and develop your personal ability to lead others. You'll grow intellectually, physically, spiritually, or socially. You'll learn the benefits of being a volunteer and develop lifelong leisure skills. Perhaps the most important benefit, however, is that you'll have a place for having fun with people you enjoy being around. Student activities, when all else is said and done, can be a wonderful release from the pressures of academics.

Campus life is radically different than it may have been for your parents. Receiving a degree no longer guarantees you a job or a bright future. Because a college degree is now the norm rather than the exception, employers are looking for other features that set you apart from other college graduates. These features may include your major, grade point, community service, and job experience, but they will surely also include your participation and leadership positions in campus activities. So stop by your student activities office on campus and find out what's of interest to you. Get involved right away, even if you have to start small. If you budget your time wisely, you may find that involvement in student activities is another tie that binds you to your college and may well help you stay on the path to success.

▌ EXERCISE 1 ▐

RELATING ACTIVITIES TO PERSONAL DEVELOPMENT

Use the six areas of personal development (social, intellectual, physical, spiritual, emotional, occupational) as a basis, and list under each area the types of activities, skills, and organizations that are designed to spur your growth in that particular developmental path. After you have done this, check your categories and determine how many organizations offer you development in at least two areas, three areas, or more.

■ EXERCISE 2

LEARNING LEADERSHIP SKILLS
FIRSTHAND

Ask your campus activities advisor which people on campus are model leaders. Contact these people and observe them in their leadership roles, then make appointments to talk with them about their leadership experience and techniques. Write a paper that describes these techniques, and then ask the president of your club or organization whether you could be allowed to chair the next meeting to experience the thrill and art of leadership.

■ EXERCISE 3

A CLASS SURVEY OF CAMPUS ACTIVITIES

If your class makes a small effort, it can compile an activities directory for every member of your group. Obtain a list of clubs and organizations from your campus activities office. Divide the list equitably among class members and assign each member the task of writing profiles of the organizations on his or her list. A profile might include size of group, major projects, interests of members, males vs. females in group, frequency of meetings, dates and times of meetings, financial obligation, and other items as you see fit. All information can be compiled into a booklet and circulated among all students, who may then use the booklet to choose organizations of interest to them.

JOURNEY FIVE

BECOMING RESPONSIBLE FOR YOUR PERSONAL GROWTH

It hardly seems possible, but we've almost reached the end of the trail. In one sense, you're nearing the end of this short book which has been designed to help you acclimate more comfortably to your initial college experience. In another sense, this is just the beginning of the road for you, and, quite frankly, it makes us almost green with envy. For we know of no other time in life when a person has so much to look forward to, so many options to choose from, and so much to learn. Don't get us wrong; we're still looking forward to new experiences, choosing from options, and we're certainly still learning—even at our ages! Nonetheless, it simply can't compare to the thrill of entering college and realizing for perhaps the first time in your life that you are going to be calling more and more of the shots from now on. It's scary, sure. But once you discover you are quite capable of making decisions, it's one of the greatest feelings in the world. We hope our suggestions have given you the confidence you may have needed to begin college with an open mind and a feeling of excitement. We hope we've helped you understand the significance and the seriousness of a college education. More than that, however, we hope we have convinced you of the importance of taking advantage of everything your college has to offer—the professors and their knowledge, to be certain; but also the hundred and one other services, organizations, and people that add zest and vitality to the college experience.

Join us now on the final step in this book. It's one that, quite logically, invites you to open a new path for the future.

STEP 19

SUCCESSFULLY COMPLETING
YOUR FRESHMAN YEAR.
OPTIONS.

Let's look into the near future. It's the end of your freshman year and you've been most successful. Taking the lead from this book, you've been able to justify your decision to attend college. You've gotten involved with a group or groups of people. You've even made friends with professors and with your academic advisor. You've practiced writing skills, checked out the helping services on campus, improved your study habits, and even investigated the career center for advice on your major and your future career. You've mastered the art of using the college library, and you've almost been able to manage your budget (at least you're not starving!). What's more, you've been practicing relaxation and assertiveness skills, and you've found that they really help make life easier. You've invested in a good exercise regimen and even made some attempt to cut down on your junk food intake. You've made a wise decision regarding alcohol, whatever that decision might be. You've worked to make your campus home a place you like to come home to, and you've gotten involved in activities on campus, even to the point of testing your skills at leadership.

Is it possible that you could have done all this in less than a year? Of course, it's possible, as long as you have confidence in your abilities, manage your time well, and never forget that classes and studies must come first. If they don't, you won't be around very long to experience all the other things a college offers.

■ THANK GOODNESS FOR OPTIONS

As you think about it, isn't it wonderful that your college or university allows you to tailor your college years to suit yourself, and doesn't force you into a pattern that may not be right for you? Come to think of it, it's these options that make it more inviting for you to achieve in college, provided you know you have options and make the most of them.

For example, you have the option of living at home, on campus, or with friends. You have a choice of academic majors, and in many cases, of elective courses within those fields of study. You have a choice of friends and mentors who can be significant individuals for you as you progress through college and life. You can choose to attend summer school, if you wish, or remain on campus in the summer and work nearby. You can seek internships in your academic field, participate in those extracurricular activities that suit your interests and skills best, and assume leadership roles in many of them. You might even decide to pursue graduate studies, or become involved in domestic or international student exchange programs which allow you to study at another college or university for a semester or two.

Your college experience may take you on trips to other parts of the country or the world, and this could affect where you choose to live after college. College may also provide options that introduce you to new interests: new sports, new cultural experiences such as theatre and music, new types of literature or magazines, and new relationships.

Options are a marvelous thing, but they're also the reason you may need to seek advice during your college years. Don't forget our recommendations about contacting the right people for that advice. If you're not certain where to begin, ask your academic advisor, provided he or she is the sort of advisor we've described in this book. Above all, never forget that college is one of the all-time great experiences of life. You can make what you will of it, but in order to get the most out of college, you have to put forth your best efforts, too.

■ SOME FINAL THOUGHTS ON SURVIVING

No one can provide you with a magic formula for surviving your freshman year, but the following recommendations come as close to that as we can find. They resulted from a rather extensive study done at Pennsylvania State University on freshmen who survived and those who didn't. We think you'll find the comments so interesting, you may wish to copy them and hang them in a prominent place in your room.[1]

■ SURVIVING YOUR FRESHMAN YEAR

According to this study, success doesn't depend on whether you're black or white, rich or poor, or whether your parents went to college. None of these seems to have anything to do with surviving your freshman year. But other things do matter. Be sure you want to come in the first place. Don't come to college simply because all your friends are going. If you have a specific vocational goal in mind, you'll be more likely to come back for your sophomore year. Uncertainty about a specific major, however, is nothing to worry about. In fact, you may be better off not having a preference for a major as a freshman, if you are unsure about it.

Whether or not you work in your freshman year won't affect your chances of survival, but how much you work does matter. The dropout rate of those who work more than 20 hours a week is five times that of those who work less than 20 hours a week. Certain types of personal problems may also affect your chances of returning for your sophomore year. If you have difficulty getting along with people, if you are lonely, if you are ill, you are more likely to drop out. So deal with little problems before they become big ones.

Live on campus. Freshmen living off campus drop out at a rate

---

1. The following comments have been adapted from "The Academic and Personal Development of Penn State Freshmen," a longitudinal study of the class of 1980, by Lee Upcraft, Patricia Peterson, and Betty Moore, Office of Residential Life Programs, Division of Student Affairs, The Pennsylvania State University. Used by permission.

nearly twice that of on-campus freshmen. Make a real effort to get along with your roommate, and try to stay with that person during your entire freshman year. But if you have irresolvable differences, request a room change because prolonged incompatibility will increase your chances of dropping out.

Most importantly, be concerned if you run into academic difficulties. As you might expect, students who are having academic difficulties are more likely to drop out than others.

■ TOWARD ACADEMIC EXCELLENCE

Succeeding in college is more than simply a matter of studying hard and applying native intelligence. You may be thinking about whether you should find a job during your freshman year. It's all right to work as long as you don't overdo it. Clearly, going to college full-time and working more than half-time is an open invitation to earning lower grades.

Maintain a good relationship with your parents. Students who have very close relationships with parents earn significantly higher grades than those who are incompatible with their parents. Don't assume that, just because you're away from home, your parents don't matter anymore.

If you get sick or injure yourself, have financial problems, or have difficulty getting along with people, you are likely to earn lower grades. We also urge you to live on campus. Freshmen who live off campus tend to earn lower grades, as a group, than freshmen living on campus. Get along with your resident assistant, for this can also lead to better grades.

■ TOWARD PERSONAL GROWTH

It's interesting to note that who you are in terms of your background and characteristics prior to entering college may have a greater effect on your personal development than anything that happens to you during your freshman year. Things such as working more than 20 hours a week and a good relationship with parents, seem to have little impact on personal development, although—as we have seen—they can affect your grades and survival rate.

Still, there are other things to watch for. Lots of traumatic events and problems in your freshman year can negatively affect your social and emotional development (illness, injury, academic difficulty, difficulty in getting along with people, loneliness, etc.). Otherwise, personal development doesn't seem to be affected by whether or not you live on campus, or how well you get along with roommates.

Remember, these are generalizations and represent the results of a study. Even so, they can help you recognize the warning signals and thereby be better prepared to alter them.

■ SETTING GOALS FOR YOUR FUTURE

Before we wind this whole thing up, we want you to attempt to write some goals for your future. It certainly isn't required that you begin college with specific goals. In fact, many people who are quite successful claim they have never concerned themselves with goals. Their successes, they claim, have come about as a natural result of their efforts. In a sense, this is what goal setting is all about. You reach a goal only by deliberately following a path toward it, and along that path you pick up the skills and experiences that bring you closer to attaining that goal. In his *Human Potential Seminar Basic Guide-Handbook,* James D. McHolland lists these criteria for setting worthwhile goals:

1. The goal is achievable. You have enough time to do the goal. You have the necessary skills, strengths, abilities, or resources.

2. It is believable and realistic for you. You believe you can achieve it, and your mental attitude is positive and optimistic.

3. You want to do it. It is not something you choose because it's required or you feel you should do it. *Want* involves satisfaction and pleasure, because it is truly your own goal.

4. Your goal has focus. It is presented without an alternative. You have made your decision.

5. It is not injurious to you or to others.

6. You are motivated to achieve the goal.

7. It is worth setting because it fits your personal value system, and it will make some difference to you if you achieve it.

8. You have set a target date for achieving your goal.[2]

Your goals also should be specific and to the point. Otherwise, they often lack the clear focus McHolland speaks of as essential to goal setting.

■ LOOKING AHEAD

Well, here we are at last. In one sense, we've about reached the end of our trip. In another, things are only beginning. The rest of college lies ahead of you, and beyond that, the rest of your life. What you do with that time, and how you feel about your accomplishments, will depend to a great extent on how you approach the next few years. We wish you our best, and remind you that taking college step by step is one way to make the most of it, as long as you make each and every step count.

┃ EXERCISE 1

SETTING GOALS FOR THE FUTURE

Using the guidelines discussed in this section, write your goals for the coming year. Keep this paper and check it at the end of the year. Continue to update it once each year until you graduate. Then keep

---

2. James D. McHolland. *Human Potential Seminar Basic Guide-Handbook*. Evanston, Ill: National Center for Human Potential Seminars & Services, 1976. Used by permission.

updating and checking it on an annual basis. Years from now, it may be interesting to see how your goals have changed—or remained the same—since your college days.

■ EXERCISE 2
A FANTASY TRIP INTO THE FUTURE

Imagine the years have gone by, and you now have a son or daughter who has just left for college. As you think about what he or she will encounter during this new experience, you decide to write a letter of advice which will reach the dormitory during the first week your teenager is there. Write this letter, including any ideas and suggestions which seem appropriate, and share the finished letter with classmates as they read theirs to the rest of the group. What does it feel like to be a parent of a college-age child? Can you speculate as to how your own parents might feel about your going to college, and whether your thoughts are similar to theirs?

GLOSSARY

FROM GPR TO SAT: A GLOSSARY OF COLLEGE JARGON

■ by Ed Ewing

One way in which college is different from other institutions is in the vocabulary used by its residents and employees. Many of the terms you'll find in your admission materials, orientation information, handbooks, and catalogs were taken from the literature of the first colleges and universities in Europe, and are used today more out of custom and tradition than for any practical reasons. This glossary takes you on a tour of the unusual language you may encounter from faculty, deans, and your college administration, and will help you understand what they mean.

To show you how difficult college jargon can be, look back at the paragraph you've just read, particularly at the terms college, university, faculty, *and* dean. *What do you think these mean? Think of a definition for each of them and compare your definitions to those you'll learn here. We'll begin by helping you with the two most difficult words,* college *and* university.

A university is a group of colleges, and the degree programs (majors) are within the various colleges. The college is the degree-granting component of a university, but different types of colleges exist. Some offer only undergraduate degrees. Some offer both undergraduate and graduate degrees, and others may offer only graduate degrees. A college of law or a law school is a primary example of this last. In the following glossary, we've tried to define some common words or terms you may encounter during your college years. We hope it will help you better understand your college life.

■ ACADEMIC ADVISOR   Colleges have many people who carry the title of advisor or counselor. Your academic advisor may be a faculty member in the academic field you've chosen or a full-time administrative employee of the school who works in a counseling office. You'll be assigned an advisor once you begin college, and this person will serve as your resource to all academic and nonacademic services. While an academic advisor will help you plan your college schedule or choose a major, they can also offer much more. Ask about anything that puzzles you, and you may save both time and money.

■ ACCREDITATION   Colleges and universities are judged, or accredited, either by an organization of other colleges and universities, or by professional organizations. Accrediting teams visit on a regular basis and judge schools on faculty, degrees offered, library facilities, laboratories, other facilities, and finances. Southern schools are accredited by the Southern Association of Colleges and Schools. A law school must be accredited by the American Bar Association. A college of business must be accredited by the American Association of Collegiate Schools of Business, and colleges of communications or journalism may be accredited by the Association for Education in Journalism and Mass Communication. You should seek accredited schools and programs since these are typically the best of their kind, and are recognized as such by many future employers.

■ ADMISSIONS   The first contact you may have with a college or university may be with its admissions office. The people who work there are trying to "sell" their school and its programs to you, and they'll send you many forms. Read these forms carefully and note all deadlines. Send your application to them early, because some schools may assign dormitory space on the basis of the date you're accepted for admission. Some schools offer more than one type of admission status. You may be permitted entrance to one college or major program, but denied entrance to another. Acceptance to a university does not always guarantee acceptance into all of its programs. See Major; Associate degree; Bachelor's degree.

■ ALUMNUS   A graduate of a college or university. Schools have alumni offices, which may ask you for money or other support after you graduate.

■ ASSISTANT PROFESSOR   See Professor.

■ ASSOCIATE DEGREE   May be an associate degree in arts or an associate degree in science (AA or AS). Although many terms used by American universities were taken from European schools, this term is apparently an exception. An associate degree is a two-year degree. Many associate degree programs are offered at community and junior colleges and at technical schools, but many large universities also offer such programs. Just because you earn an associate degree does not mean you're halfway toward a bachelor's degree. Some states have agreements that require state colleges and universities to accept all classes satisfactorily completed toward an associate degree, and to count those credits toward a bachelor's degree. This is not true in all states, however.

■ ASSOCIATE PROFESSOR   See Professor.

■ BACHELOR'S DEGREE   The formal name for a four-year college degree. Two major types are the Bachelor of Arts (BA) and Bachelor of Science (BS). Requirements for these degrees vary, depending on the standards of the school or college.

■ BOOKSTORE   More than a place that sells textbooks, a college bookstore may also sell running shorts, pens and pencils, greeting cards, and a host of other items. Be certain you purchase the proper edition of required texts, and see if used copies are available at a reduced price. Always keep your book receipt, and do not mark in the book until you're sure you'll keep it, or you may have trouble obtaining a refund. Bookstores are usually located in student centers or college/university unions.

■ CAFETERIA OR DINING HALL   These terms mean the same thing on some campuses but different things on others. The dining hall may be part of a dormitory, and your food may be prepaid if you purchased a meal card or board plan. A cafeteria is a place where you pay for each item you select; it may be located in the student center.

■ CAREER COUNSELING/PLANNING   Most campuses began offering this service in the 1970s because students saw a direct relationship between what they were studying in college and the job market. Students wanted to know where the jobs were, and what they needed to achieve to be eligible for them. Career planning services include but are not limited to: self-assessment and interest tests, job search workshops, decision-making workshops, and résumé workshops. These services are usually located in counseling centers, student affairs offices, or placement offices.

■ CARREL   A study room or numbered desk and chair in the college library that can be assigned to students. Not everyone is eligible for one, and you must request a carrel from the college librarian.

■ CHANCELLOR   Title given to a high academic officer at some colleges and universities. The chancellor is usually just below the president in importance.

■ CLASS CARD OR COURSE CARD   Usually required for registration unless you register by computer. At registration, you pick up one card for each class approved for you by your advisor. The card usually lists the name and number of the class, number of credits, days, times, and name of the professor. If more than one section of the same course is offered, a section number will appear. *Always check your course cards carefully.* Once these cards are fed into the computer, you are assigned a seat in the class, and your name will appear on the class roll for the card that you submit. See Section.

■ CLASS STANDING   Most colleges link your standing to the number of hours you've earned, not the number of years you've attended school. A freshman is enrolled in the first quarter of college work. A sophomore is in the second quarter. A junior has passed the halfway point, and a senior has three-fourths of his or her requirements completed. This rule applies to students on the quarter and semester systems in four-year undergraduate progrms. See Quarter system and Semester system.

■ CLEP   Stands for College Level Examination Program, a series of tests you may take to demonstrate proficiency in various college subjects. If you pass the test, you will earn credit for certain college courses. CLEP subject exams cover individual courses, such as Introductory Psychology; CLEP general exams incorporate several courses, such as the one for social studies. Be aware that some colleges will accept CLEP subject exams, but not CLEP general exams. CLEP tests are usually administered through the college testing office. You can also obtain information about CLEP tests from your admissions office and/or your advisor.

■ COEDUCATIONAL   A school that admits men and women. Most colleges are coeducational. Some schools even have coeducational residence halls where men and women live in the same building, but not in the same room.

■ COGNATE   A group of courses related to a student's major and approved by his or her advisor. Such courses are required for graduation at many colleges. Cognates are junior and senior level courses. Colleges that don't require a cognate may require a minor. See Minor.

■ COMMENCEMENT   A day set aside by colleges to award degrees to graduating students. Some schools hold two or three commencements annually, but the most popular ones are held in May or early June.

■ COMMUNITY COLLEGE   A two-year college that may also be known as a junior college or technical school. These colleges award associate degrees, and technical colleges may offer other types of degrees or certificates as well. Be certain that the community college you select is accredited, and remember that there's no guarantee that all courses you take at a two-year college will transfer to a four-year college or university.

■ COMPREHENSIVE EXAMINATION   Some schools use this term to describe final exams, which are given during the last days of the term. The word *comprehensive* means that all material covered during the term may be included on the exam. Graduate students may also take comprehensive exams to earn the master's or doctoral degree.

■ CONTINUING EDUCATION   Over the years, the meaning of this term has changed. Some schools may still refer to such programs as "adult education." Continuing education programs enable the nontraditional college student to take classes without having to be admitted as a degree candidate. While continuing education students may take college courses for credit, some colleges have established noncredit learning programs under this name.

■ CORE COURSES/DISTRIBUTION REQUIREMENTS/BASIC REQUIREMENTS/ GENERAL EDUCATION   These terms all mean the same thing. Colleges require that all students complete specific groups of courses. These courses usually occur at the freshman and sophomore levels and include English, math, science, and history requirements. Since many of these lower numbered courses must be completed before other courses can be taken, it's wise to complete your core courses as early as possible. See Prerequisite.

■ COUNSELING OFFICE   Counseling is provided by trained professionals at your college. Counselors can help you with various adjustment problems and may refer you to other services. There are many types of counselors; you'll find them in the following offices: Admissions, Financial Aid, Residence Halls, Career Planning, Placement, Veterans' Affairs, Study Skills, Academic Advising, and Counseling Centers. Counselors treat in confidence whatever you tell them. Once you determine that you need some type of counseling, seek it out. Your tuition is paying for it.

■ COURSE NUMBER   Different colleges number their courses in different ways. Most undergraduates take courses at the 100 level through at least the 400 level, but this will vary on different campuses. Graduate level courses carry higher numbers. The 100-level courses are usually survey courses which introduce that subject, while upper-level courses may spend an entire term covering a narrower topic in more detail. Some 100-level courses must be completed before you may take upper-level work in that subject. Check your catalog and ask your advisor for help.

■ CREDIT HOUR   See Quarter/Semester hour.

■ CURRICULUM   All courses required for your degree. Some colleges refer to all courses in the catalog as the curriculum, and many schools provide students with curriculum outlines or curriculum sheets in addition to the catalog. These sheets show what courses you must take and may indicate the order in which you must take them. The latter is called "course sequencing."

■ DEAN   A college administrator who may have been a professor. Some deans are academic deans, which means they head colleges. Some colleges and universities have a dean of student affairs and a dean of business affairs. The academic dean is a person who oversees your degree program. He or she can grant exceptions to academic policy. The other types of deans are executives who may or may not work directly with students, although most work in the student services area. Some deans may have associate or assistant deans to help them.

■ DEAN'S LIST   If you make high grades, you'll make the Dean's List at the end of the term. This is an academic honor and looks good on your résumé and on applications for graduate study. See what your school requires for you to make the list, and make it as many times as you can.

■ DEFICIENCY   Another word that can mean more than one thing. You may be told you have a one-course deficiency that you must make up before graduation or entrance to a particular program. Your grades may be fine, but the deficiency exists as a prerequisite for what you want to do. Deficiency can also mean that your grades are so low that you may not be permitted to return to school.

■ DEPARTMENT   A college is often organized into academic departments. For example, a group of history faculty will develop a curriculum for students studying history. The history department will offer all history courses for every student at the school, including history majors.

■ DISMISSAL   At most schools, dismissal means the same thing as suspension, and you will be told to leave the school for academic or disciplinary reasons. College catalogs explain the circumstances for dismissal, and you should learn these rules and obey them. Dismissal or suspension usually is noted on your official record or transcript, and the requirements to reenter college will vary. See Leave of absence and Probation.

■ DISSERTATION   One of the final requirements for the highest academic degree a student can earn in most fields, the doctorate or Ph.D. In some fields, the dissertation is book length. The graduate student is expected to break new ground in research and must defend her or his dissertation before a faculty committee. See Graduate student.

■ DOCTORAL DEGREE   Requires additional years of study beyond the bachelor's and/or master's degrees, and is awarded upon successful completion of course work, the dissertation, and orals. Most of your professors probably have a Ph.D. (doctor of philosophy), but other types, including the M.D. (medical doctor) and J.D. (doctor of jurisprudence) also require extensive study.

■ DORMITORY   See Residence hall.

■ DROP   Most colleges allow students to drop courses without penalty during specified periods of time. Dropping a course can be dangerous if you don't know the proper procedures, since you'll need to complete certain forms and obtain official signatures. If you're receiving financial aid, your status may change if you drop a course. Finally, dropping courses certainly will affect your graduation date.

■ ELECTIVES   Students who say, "I think I'll take an elective course," may think that electives differ from other course requirements. This is only partially true, for electives are required for graduation for most college degrees. An elective is a course you may select from an academic area of interest to you. The course will not count in your core, major, or minor/cognate. Each college decides the number of electives you may take, and you may take them at any time. Consult your advisor, and see if he or she recommends that you complete core courses before choosing electives.

■ EVALUATION OF COURSES   See Validation of credits.

■ EXTRACURRICULAR (COCURRICULAR)   A word describing activities, clubs, or organizations you may join and participate in, above and beyond your academic courses. Such activities provide fun and friends, and also look good on your résumé, but keep in mind that some are more valuable than others. Ask a counselor for advice, since certain activities may lead you into career choices. Activities include student government, student media, clubs, volunteer work, and faculty/student committees.

■ FACULTY   All the teachers at your college. The names of faculty positions and the ranks held by individuals will vary. See Professor.

■ FEES   At most colleges, fees are costs that are required in addition to tuition, Fees may be charged for housing, health, labs, parking, and many other things. Most college catalogs give a good idea of what fees you'll have to pay and when you must pay them. See Tuition.

■ FINAL EXAMS   Some schools call them comprehensive exams and hold them during an examination week, a period when your instructors may find out how much you've learned from them. Most finals are written rather than oral. Professors usually tell students about finals near the beginning of the term, and not all professors require them. A final may count as much as one-half of your grade, or it could count much less. Some schools may also schedule midterm exams.

■ FINANCIAL AID   A complicated subject in recent years. See Step 13. Most colleges have a financial aid office to provide information to students on scholarships, grants, loans, and so on. Some forms of financial aid are gifts, but others are loans that must be repaid with interest. Some aid is offered only to new freshmen, and you must apply before college begins to be eligible. Many grants and loans are provided through federal government assistance, and government regulations control this money. To determine your eligibility for any sort of aid, see your financial aid counselor as early as you can.

■ FRATERNITY   See Greeks.

■ FULL-TIME STUDENT   Students enrolled for a specified number of hours, such as twelve semester hours or more. At most schools, part-time students receive the same benefits as full-time students. At others, part-time students may receive limited health care and no athletic tickets. Ask your advisor about the advantages of going full-time, but remember, if you must work, raise a family, or handle other obligations, a part-time program may be the more sensible one to pursue.

■ GRADE-POINT AVERAGE (GPA)   Sometimes called the cumulative average or grade-point ratio (GPR). Most colleges base grades on a 4-point scale, with points assigned to each grade (A = 4, B = 3, C = 2, D = 1, F = 0). To compute your GPA for one term, you need only complete three simple mathematical steps: multiply, add, divide. *Multiply* the number of points representing the grade you receive for each course times the number of credit hours for the course. *Add* the points for all courses to determine the total number of points you've earned for the term. *Divide* the total points by the number of credit hours you attempted that term. The result will be your GPA. Some colleges complicate this with a 3-point system or by using grades in addition to A through F. College catalogs show you how the system works at individual schools.

■ GRADES OR GRADING SYSTEM   Most schools use the A through F system. A is the highest grade and F means failure. A through D are passing grades for which you will earn points and credits. If you ever transfer colleges, however, the D grades may not transfer. D's and F's are bad because most colleges require a minimum 2.0 GPA or C average for graduation, and you might lose financial aid, housing, and other benefits when your GPA falls below a certain level. Bad grades and low GPAs also lead to dismissal or suspension. Some schools have a pass/fail grade (P/F or S/U) and an incomplete grade (I), the latter representing work not completed during the term it was taken. Learning the grading system of your college is one of your first assignments.

■ GRADUATE STUDENT   A person who has earned at least a bachelor's degree (B.A. or B.S.), and is presently enrolled in a program granting a master's degree (M.A. or M.S.) and/or a doctorate (Ph.D.). Students in law school, medical school, and other specialized programs beyond the bachelor's level are also classified as graduate students.

■ GREEKS   Used to describe students who join fraternities or sororities. Discuss the possibility of becoming a Greek with someone whose opinions you value.

■ HIGHER EDUCATION   Any college courses you take or any degree you earn after completing high school (secondary education). Also called postsecondary education.

■ HONORS   Most colleges recognize good grades in the form of academic honors. Dean's List is the most common award. Honors are also awarded at graduation to superior students, and the following Latin words are used: *cum laude* (with praise), *magna cum laude* (with great praise), *summa cum laude* (with highest praise).

■ HOURS   Another word for credits. If you enroll for fifteen hours this term and pass all five of your three-hour courses, you'll earn fifteen credits. There is often a relationship between the number of hours you spend in the classroom each week and the number of credits you can earn from the course. After you accumulate the proper number of credits/hours, you will graduate with an associate or bachelor's degree.

■ INCOMPLETE   See Grades or grading system.

■ INDEPENDENT STUDY   Can mean at least two things. An independent study course is one in which you complete course requirements on your own time, under the direction of a professor, and in a nonclassroom setting. This term may also describe some work you've done, either by yourself or with others, that is creative and that shows your ability to work with minimal direction.

■ INSTRUCTOR   See Professor.

■ INTERNSHIP   An arrangement that permits students to work and receive college credit in their major. Internships are required for graduation in some fields, such as psychology, nursing, and medicine. Prerequisites must be completed before you may take an internship, and you must complete an application and obtain the proper signatures before you will be allowed to intern.

■ JUNIOR   See Class standing.

■ JUNIOR COLLEGE   See Community college.

■ LABORATORIES   Many science courses come with laboratories. Many large universities call other learning experiences "laboratories." For example, courses in foreign language, computer science, education, psychology, and journalism may have labs. Many courses require labs whether you want to take the lab or not, but in other cases labs may be optional. Check your catalog to see what labs are in store for you.

■ LEAVE OF ABSENCE   Another way to say you've withdrawn completely from college. Most students take a leave of absence while still in good academic standing, with the intention of seeking readmittance at a later date. Remember to read the rules and regulations in your catalog, since colleges have different ideas about the meaning of a leave of absence.

■ LECTURER   See Professor.

■ LOWER DIVISION   Many colleges and universities have divided their academic programs into lower and upper divisions (also called pre-professional and professional). Your standing depends on the number of hours you've accumulated, prerequisites completed, forms completed and signed, and grade-point average. Students in the upper division usually enjoy greater privileges and certainly are closer to graduation.

■ MAJOR   Your field of specialization in college. As much as 30 percent of the courses you need for graduation may fall into this category. Major courses usually carry higher course numbers. Your advisor will explain the requirements of your major to you.

■ MASTER SCHEDULE   See Schedule of classes.

■ MASTER'S DEGREE STUDENTS   Students who have chosen to continue their education in either a Master of Arts (M.A.) or Master of Science (M.S.) program. Master's students may have entered a different program from the one in which they earned their bachelor's degree. Comprehensive exams, a thesis, and/or practicums and internships may be required. See Thesis.

■ MATRICULATE   An uncommon, admissions office term that means you've applied for a degree program, have been accepted in that program, and have enrolled for classes. At that point, you're considered matriculated.

■ MINOR   A group of courses that may or may not be required for your degree. Not all colleges require a minor. Your advisor may tell you that your minor must be "academically related" to your major, as government is to history. Minors may also consist of courses taken in a professional school, such as business administration.

■ ORAL   An examination during which your professor will ask you questions about your class and you will answer aloud. Undergraduate students usually don't have to undergo orals.

■ ORIENTATION   Most colleges now set aside a single day, several days, or even longer for orientation. During this period, new students and their parents are introduced to academic programs, facilities, and services provided by the college. Orientation may also include academic advisement and preregistration for classes.

■ PART-TIME STUDENT   See Full-time student.

■ PASS/FAIL OR PASS/NO PASS OR SATISFACTORY/UNSATISFACTORY   Many
colleges allow you to take certain courses on a pass/fail system. By
passing the course, you will earn credits toward graduation, but the
grade will not count in your GPA. Pass/fail grades do not have grade
points assigned to them. Most schools will not allow you to take core
courses, major courses, or minor/cognate courses on this system, but
may allow free electives as pass/fail options. To take courses pass/fail,
you must fill out the proper forms before the established deadline in
the term.

■ PLACEMENT   Several definitions are appropriate here. Placement tests
tell academic departments what level of knowledge you've achieved in
their subject. A college placement office can help you in résumé writing and interviewing. This office may, with your permission, keep a job
file on you and release information to prospective employers upon
request. Recruiters from business and industry often recruit graduating
seniors and graduate students through college placement offices.

■ PRACTICUM   Generally, a practicum experience covers a limited
amount of material in depth, rather than trying, as an internship does,
to provide an overview of an area. The terms may be used in-
terchangeably, however, and refer to practical types of learning experiences, usually for college credit.

■ PREREGISTRATION   Many colleges employ preregistration systems
(often computer-assisted) to simplify the process of signing up for
courses. Preregistration usually occurs in the middle of the term prior
to the one you're registering for. This early registration also tells colleges what courses students want, when they'll want them, and what
professors they request. Preregistration gives students a greater chance
of receiving the courses and sections asked for.

■ PREREQUISITE   A prerequisite is a course or courses that must be
completed as a condition for taking another course. Catalogs state prerequisites. Often a GPA or class standing may constitute a prerequisite
for certain classes.

■ PRESIDENT   The chief executive officer of the university or college.
Presidents report directly to governing boards (trustees). Unless you
attend a small school, you won't see this person very often, except at
official functions such as commencement.

■ PROBATION   A warning that you are not making satisfactory academic
progress toward your degree. Probation is followed by suspension/

dismissal unless the situation is corrected. Probation may also exist for disciplinary reasons.

■ PROFESSOR   College teachers are ranked as teaching assistant, instructor, lecturer, or professor. Professor is the highest rank and includes three levels: assistant professor, associate professor, and (full) professor. To avoid confusion, note how your teacher introduces himself or herself the first day of class. When in doubt, use "professor." While most professors have earned a doctoral degree, this is not a rigid rule for holding professorial rank.

■ PROFICIENCY EXAM   A test used to measure whether or not you've reached a certain level of knowledge. Such exams may allow you to exempt, with or without credit, certain lower level courses. Math and foreign language departments make use of proficiency exams.

■ QUARTER HOUR   A unit of credit given at colleges whose terms are called quarters, which last approximately ten weeks. See Semester hour.

■ QUARTER SYSTEM   Colleges operating on this system have four terms, or quarters: fall, winter, spring, and summer. If you attend full-time and plan to finish in four years without attending summer school, you'll take courses for twelve quarters. See Semester system.

■ REGISTRAR   The college administrator who maintains your transcript, directs the registration process, and performs other academic duties as assigned by the faculty. When faculty submit final grades, the registrar posts them to your transcript, and mails you a copy.

■ REGISTRATION   The act of scheduling your classes for each term. Whether you preregister or sign up just prior to the term, you should seek academic advisement first to be certain you're taking the proper courses. When in doubt, ask your advisor first! See Preregistration.

■ REINSTATEMENT OR READMISSION   A return to college following suspension or a leave of absence; you must apply for reinstatement or readmission. In some cases you'll be readmitted with no restrictions. If your GPA is low, you may be readmitted on probation. Check the academic regulations at your school.

■ RESIDENCE HALL   A fancy term for dormitory, a residence hall is operated by the college as student housing. Ask your residence hall or dorm counselor to explain the rules that apply to your place of residence on campus.

■ RESIDENCY   State-supported colleges and universities charge a high-er tuition to students who do not reside (maintain residency) the year around in the same state and who are not considered legal residents of that state. If you live in the same state in which you attend college, you have residency in that state, and are eligible for in-state tuition, provided you meet other specific requirements of your school.

■ SABBATICAL   A period of paid or semi-paid vacation awarded every six or seven years to professors, who are expected, during this time, to conduct academic research or writing that makes a contribution to their academic discipline.

■ SCHEDULE OF CLASSES   Also called a master schedule, this is a listing of all classes that will be offered during the coming term, including days and times of class meetings, name of instructor, building and room, and other registration information.

■ SCHOLARSHIP   A financial award made for academic achievement. Many scholarships are reserved for new freshmen, and may be re-newed annually, provided grades are satisfactory. The money is applied to tuition.

■ SECTION   The different classes offered for a single subject. For ex-ample, a large college might offer fifty different sections of freshman English. Depending on the section you register for, you may have a different teacher, different textbook, and different meeting time than your friends who are taking different sections of the same course.

■ SEMESTER HOUR   The unit of credit you earn for course work that takes a semester to complete. Many college courses carry three credits, or semester hours.

■ SEMESTER SYSTEM   As opposed to the quarter system, a semester sys-tem consists of a fall semester, a spring semester, and summer school. A full-time student can complete a bachelor's degree in eight semesters without attending summer school.

■ SEMINAR   A class containing fewer students than a lecture class, in which the teacher leads discussions and all students participate. The majority of classes in graduate school are operated this way, although you'll find seminars in undergraduate programs as well.

■ SENIOR   See Class standing.

■ SOPHOMORE   See Class standing.

■ SORORITY   See Greeks.

■ SPECIAL STUDENT   In most colleges, this is a student who has not matriculated (has not been accepted into a degree program). A special student may have one degree, but may wish to continue his or her education by selecting courses without regard to a degree program. Military personnel are often admitted as special students. Special students may be exempted from certain prerequisites, but they can't receive financial aid or free athletic tickets.

■ STUDENT TEACHING   An internship that all education majors must complete before graduation.

■ STUDENT UNION   A building, also called the student center, where you can eat, see a movie, meet friends, and take part in extracurricular activities.

■ SUMMER SESSION (SUMMER SCHOOL)   For students who wish to make up deficiencies, get ahead, or just can't seem to get enough of school. Classes meet every day for longer periods than during the regular sessions. Since things move quickly, good academic advisement is essential before you consider summer school. You may also take summer courses as a transient student at another school, provided your advisor has given you prior approval. Since many schools will not let you take courses you failed at another school, be careful.

■ SUSPENSION   See Dismissal.

■ SYLLABUS   One or more pages of class requirements a professor will give you on the first day. The syllabus acts as a course outline, telling when you must complete assignments, readings, and so on. A professor may also include on the syllabus her or his grading system, attendance policy, and a brief description of the course. Be sure you get one and use it.

■ TECHNICAL (TECH) SCHOOLS   Technical education systems established by many states offer specialized two-year degrees and certificates. While these schools may be accredited, course work may be so technically oriented that it won't transfer to a bachelor's degree program. If you plan to attend a TECH school, be certain to ask about the "college parallel curriculum." See Associate degree.

■ TERM PAPER   Not all college courses require one, but when you're assigned a term paper, you should treat it as a very important portion of the course. The instructor may give you the entire term to research and write a term paper; hence, its name. Be certain you know which style manual your teacher prefers, and footnote accordingly.

■ THESIS   A longer research paper, usually written as partial fulfill-
ment of the requirements for a master's degree. Some schools still require a senior thesis of graduating students.

■ TRANSCRIPT   The official record of your college work, which is
maintained and updated each term by the registrar. Your courses,
grades, GPA, and graduation information will be included in your transcript.

■ TRANSFER CREDIT   If you should transfer from one college or university to another, the number of courses the new college accepts and
counts toward your degree are your transfer credits.

■ TRANSIENT STUDENT   A student who receives permission from his or
her regular college to take courses (usually in the summer) from another college.

■ TUITION   The money you pay for your college courses. See Fees.

■ UPPER DIVISION   The opposite of lower division and much closer to
graduation. See Lower division.

■ VALIDATION OF CREDITS   Procedure in which a school determines
which credits from another school may be transferred. Despite good
grades, not all of your courses may be accepted. A grade of D normally will not transfer. If you ever consider transferring from one college
to another, it's your responsibility to learn which courses and grades
will transfer.

■ WITHDRAW   Although you may withdraw from one course, this term
usually denotes the dropping of all courses for one term and leaving
school for whatever reasons you may have. Withdrawal requires a form
and signatures, and if you don't follow the prescribed procedure, you
may receive failing grades on all courses, which could place you on
academic suspension. Withdrawal in good academic standing, following
established procedures, will allow you to request readmission later.
See Reinstatement or readmission and Leave of absence.

*So there you have it: a comprehensive glossary of the many un-
familiar terms you'll be hearing during your next four years in
college. Now go back to the first paragraph of this glossary and
reread it. It should make more sense to you than it did the first
time around. In the future, you'll want to begin using these
terms in conversations about college. When someone asks,
"What did you mean by that word?" you'll be able to explain
with confidence!*

To the owner of this book:

We hope that you enjoyed *Step by Step to College Success* and found it helpful. We would like to know as much about your experience as you would care to offer. Only through your comments can we learn how to make this a better book for future readers. Thank you!

Your school: _____

Your instructor: _____

Department of: _____

Course title: _____

What did you like most about *Step by Step to College Success?* _____

_____

_____

What did you like least about it? _____

_____

_____

Was the entire book assigned for you to read? _____

If not, what parts or chapters were not assigned? _____

If you have any other comments, we'd like to hear them. Thanks!

A. Jerome Jewler   John N. Gardner

Optional:

Your Name _____   Date _____

May Wadsworth quote you in the promotion for *Step by Step to College Success?*

Yes __ No __

FOLD HERE

FOLD HERE

||||||

BUSINESS REPLY MAIL

First Class   Permit No. 34   Belmont, CA

POSTAGE WILL BE PAID BY ADDRESSEE

WADSWORTH PUBLISHING COMPANY
Ten Davis Drive
Belmont, California 94002